Code Red: The Silent Emergency

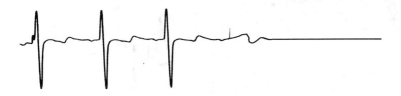

A Raw, Unforgettable Look Inside America's Medical System

May 1995

Mandana,

You are a powerful,
beautiful woman. I
love having you as a
friend.

Syd

Code Red: The Silent Emergency

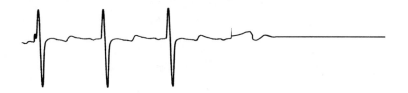

Sydne Johansen

Northwest Publishing, Inc.
Salt Lake City, Utah

Code Red: The Silent Emergency

All rights reserved.
Copyright © 1995 Sydne Johansen

For information address: Northwest Publishing, Inc.
6906 South 300 West, Salt Lake City, Utah 84047
B.K. 9-16-94
Edited by: C.D. Allen

PRINTING HISTORY
First Printing 1995

ISBN: 1-56901-744-1

NPI books are published by Northwest Publishing, Incorporated,
6906 South 300 West, Salt Lake City, Utah 84047.
The name "NPI" and the "NPI" logo are trademarks belonging to
Northwest Publishing, Incorporated.

PRINTED IN THE UNITED STATES OF AMERICA.
10 9 8 7 6 5 4 3 2 1

For my father,
who was a natural medicine man,
and for nurses, because
they bring love, compassion,
and the possibility of health
and well-being to the medical industry.

Table of Contents

Author's Note

This is a true story, an account of my experiences as a registered nurse, working in a large teaching hospital on the West Coast.

Only the names have been changed to protect the innocent and the not so innocent. Any resemblance of a name to that of a real person or hospital is entirely accidental.

That the location happens to be on the West Coast is immaterial. The experiences and stories in this book are in every hospital in every city in this country.

Preface

I have written this book because I can no longer stand by and watch medicine and nursing as it is practiced today. In this book I'm addressing issues that are rarely spoken about, that are kept secret, covered up, and protected by every level of operation in our health care system. *Code Red: The Silent Emergency* will upset you. This book is a slam against the medical industry. It may sound like my own personal rainstorm; it is not. Thousands of people could have written this book. In fact, I have been waiting for someone else to write what I have written. I haven't found it in print, so here it is. I have spoken with nurses from Seattle, Los Angeles, Chicago, Alberquerque, New York, New Orleans, and Miami over the past year. They have all encouraged me and celebrated someone finally telling this story.

With regards to our medical system, as a culture we need to be woken up and sometimes that involves shock treatment. What you are about to read is not pretty, but it is what is going on today and every day in health care facilities across this country. My intention is to bring to light what many people are not aware of. Only by getting this conversation out into our culture can change come about. After you read this book, it will be up to you. You will make the difference, our medical system will not. When we begin demanding change from the conservative, big business of medicine, it will happen.

First, I want to acknowledge the miracles of modern medicine, from the first big breakthrough of physicians washing their hands between patients, to antibiotics, open-heart surgery, organ transplants, MRIs, and the high-technology life support systems now available. This book is not meant to discount these advancements or the doctors and nurses who practice with commitment and integrity. Rather, it is meant to expose some of the horrors of our health care system that most of us do not know about and won't want to believe.

Over the last twenty to thirty years technology has advanced much more quickly than have our questions, answers, and choices on responsibility, ethics, principles, trust, living, and dying. Given this gap, doctors, hospitals, and the health care industry stepped in and began dictating our lives and deaths, in one way or another making victims of us all, and charging us exorbitant, unbelievable prices for the privilege of their services.

Although this book is certainly an assault on medicine as it is practiced today, it is written out of my love for people and for life. Though the medical industry and some politicians will dispute this book, it is written to support people in their health and well-being and has no regard for protecting a dangerous medical system.

Sydne Johansen

As I watch our government struggle with health care reform, I am captivated by the doctors defending themselves, defending the medical system, defending their six-figure and higher incomes, defending the millions of unnecessary surgeries performed every year and the billions of dollars of prescription drugs they prescribe each year. The amount of money being spent by the AMA and insurance and drug companies simply to defend and keep medicine as it is is nothing short of astounding.

This book is meant to thrust your health and well-being back into your own hands; to have you stop blindly trusting health-care workers and facilities, many of which have become monsters and parasites of a huge bureaucracy that is not working and has not worked for decades.

This book is not an attempt to undermine the authority of physicians and our health-care system; it is meant to provide a step toward ending it.

Acknowledgments

It is amazing writers have any friends left by the time they finish a book. I had no idea of the solitude it would take or the long hours in local libraries; I was unavailable for anything that didn't have to do with the writing. So many people have contributed to this book, which I could never have written without all the love and support I have received.

For all the people in the *Excellence: From Complaint to Possibility* seminar—thank you for your powerful, active listening when I declared this book into existence.

Amador Amor, Lauren, and Peter, thank you for your unconditional love, support, and encouragement.

Jennifer, thank you for being there and listening to me complain when I wanted to stop this project, and then pushing me back into action.

Laurie Parker, your patience in going through stacks and stacks of my notes and organizing them made this book come to life. Thank you.

Thank you, Carol Zizzo-Sherrard, Alison West, and Blair Henry for surrounding me with high-tech equipment: the typewriter, computer, and printer!

Henriette and Jim, this book might not have happened without your phenomenal seminar and your coaching.

Many people supported me by reading portions of this book and offering their coaching and insights. I hope that each of you will find yourselves within the text. Russ Frankenfeld, Beth and Dan Piekarsky, William Collier, JoEllen Pasman, Bob Scheck, Jennifer, Mark, Diana (aka Sam) Hunter, Jim Bergquist, Betty, Lauren Ciminera, Terry Ahern, Jorge Marrero, Gary Moskowitz, Ellen Gauthier, Kaaren, Steven Zapiler, Brian Read, Carol Zizzo-Sherrard, and Alison West— I love you, too! Here's to transforming our medical culture now. Thank you for our partnership.

Thanks also to Clara, an eighty-one-year-old retired registered nurse, and Geneva Burgess, who championed this book from the moment I declared it. Your love, prayers, and enthusiasm have made a big difference every single day.

Finally, to my partners at Northwest Publishing who had the foresight and the courage to take on this book—thank you. Christine Allen, thank you for you painstaking care in editing the words and ideas in this book, for your support, and for your love.

Prologue

On a warm Indian-summer day, I said good-bye once more to everyone I had worked with in the intensive care unit, walked out of the unit, and left the hospital as a registered nurse for the last time. After five-plus years of college and training, I was leaving nursing less than seven years into a profession in which I had planned to spend my life. Even more surprising to me was that I had lasted about two years longer than the average length of time nurses stay in that profession.

I remember, while driving home, wondering what had happened. Where had the joy, love, and passion gone? I had always thought of myself as irrepressible. Walking into my home, I headed straight for the bathroom. I took off my white uniform and shoes, hesitated for a moment, then threw them into the garbage. I stepped into the shower, somehow thinking

I could just wash away the years of frustration and outrage.

Though I wouldn't have said it this way back then, I was leaving the world of health care for reasons of integrity, or rather because of the lack of integrity within that industry. I was tired of beating my head against the brick walls of an ice-cold bureaucracy, shocked and angered by mistake after mistake made by doctors (some who were addicted to drugs and alcohol, others who were just plain incompetent), and having those mistakes immediately covered up, weary from arguing for death with dignity, sick of an arrogant, patriarchal, condescending, good-ole-boy network, and no longer willing to participate in the horrifying, unethical, dangerous mess of America's revered health-care system.

Every creative act involves…a new innocence of perception, liberated from the cataract of accepted belief.
Arthur Koestler
The Sleepwalkers

One

NURSING: A CALL TO SERVICE

I think most of us are looking for a calling, not a job. Most of us, like the assembly-line worker, have jobs that are too small for our spirit. Jobs are not big enough for people.

Studs Terkel

After years of training and studying, it seemed to happen suddenly. Just before graduating from nursing school, with state boards a few weeks away, I walked into what I considered the best hospital in the city and within thirty minutes was hired as a graduate nurse.

I remember feeling nervous and vulnerable reporting for duty the first day. Carrying around several pounds of textbooks and notebooks day after day had become a sort of security blanket and here I was walking into work with just a stethoscope. Could I really remember everything, or anything? I took a deep breath and let it out just before the elevator door opened onto the seventh floor. The floor plan was familiar after a three-month rotation through the hospital as a student nurse, so I walked quickly to the nurses' report room, hoping my mentor, Judy, would already be there. Much to my relief she was there. Judy was a great teacher, and we became a good team. We spent six weeks together, with her teaching, watching, and supervising me, then giving me more and more freedom. I loved the interaction with the patients, the team-work between the nurses, and adjusted to doing meticulous charting. Before I knew it, I was on my own.

One day after work an envelope with my state board results was in the mailbox. It had been several weeks since the exam, which was given over three full days. Though I felt I had passed every area, there was no way to be sure until the results were in my hand in black and white. I waited to open it until I got back into the house and sat down. The palms of my hands were sweaty, my knees were shaking, and my heart was racing. Years of studying were coming down to this moment. Finally, I grabbed my letter opener, took a deep breath, and pulled out the results. I did it! I passed every area! I screamed, threw the paper with the results into the air, picked up the phone and called everyone I knew. The next morning I proudly handed over my test scores to my nursing supervisor. I was an RN—it was now official.

My dream of being a nurse had started when I was about seven years old. My favorite aunt, Arlene, was a nurse. She was smart, beautiful, fun to be with, and she loved me. Arlene commuted between Seattle and Honolulu, living and working in both places. She loved her life and her career. I thought she was very worldly. I got my first suntan laying out on a beach with her. To this day I remember, every five minutes or so, asking her if I was brown yet—she was always patient with me. I still have home movies of the two of us in grass skirts and fresh flower leis from Honolulu, doing the hula together.

I was a shy, serious girl, raised in wide open spaces. In addition to the gift of life, my parents raised me with Puget Sound and the Olympic Mountains on one side of me, and acres of land and the Cascade mountain range, with Mt. Rainier, on the other side. I spent a lot of time outdoors and grew up in awe of nature.

When I was fourteen I was learning how to drive my brothers' motorcycle. I decided I already knew how and took it off a jump we had just built. As the bike left the jump, it flipped and it landed on me, crushing my left hip. I was in shock and my parents didn't wait for an ambulance. They were afraid I would die. They got me onto a plywood board, loaded me into the back of a neighbors' station wagon, and rushed me to the hospital.

For the next three months I was flat on my back, twenty-four hours a day in the hospital. As I healed I used the time to read and to make friends with all the doctors, nurses, and roommates I had.

Ninety days after the accident the doctors gave the order for me to start retraining for walking. I was to practice sitting up, standing, then walking with a walker. On that day I discovered I had no muscles left to support me doing anything but lying flat on my back. I was shocked and scared, but very determined. Several days later I was able to walk across my hospital room and just barely make it back to my bed, with the support of a walker and a nurse. Every muscle in my body was shaking, and I was drenched in sweat. As I collapsed on the edge of my bed I started crying because I was so weak and exhausted. Marilyn, my nurse, looked at me and said, "Stand up, you got to do that two more times before you even think of getting back into bed, and within two or three days you're going to be walking the length of the hallway." I looked at her like she was the nastiest witch I could imagine, got up, and made the walk two more times. I will never forget the nurses cheering me on as I ventured farther and farther down the corridors with my walker. I will never forget how I cried and they cried as they gave me a huge going-home party, telling me I was their favorite teenager in the history of the hospital, that they loved me and would miss me, while pushing me out the door to go home. Those nurses are with me today, like it all happened yesterday. They, and my aunt Arlene, are why I became a nurse.

Within days after being admitted into the hospital, the

doctors surrounded my bed, with my parents there as well, to tell me I would never walk again or be able to have children. Weeks later they adjusted their prognosis to tell me that if I did walk it would be with a severe limp. If I limp now, no one has ever brought it to my attention. I also have two healthy children. I had been faced with formidable circumstances at fourteen and had triumphed. I learned at a young age that the human spirit is powerful, and the human body resilient. I also learned to trust myself, knowing on some level how much I was capable of and how much we are all capable of, and not to pay attention to conversations, comments, or a prognosis that did not empower me.

It wasn't until recently, when I recalled this accident, that I could definitively articulate my dissatisfaction with our medical system. For several years I watched what happened to people from the moment they came through the front door of a health care facility until their release. Their experiences and my experience had me constantly questioning what I was doing as a registered nurse, questioning the medical system, our pat answers and treatments, the surgeries and the drugs. I found myself working inside a paradigm where I was wrong, the patients were wrong, and the doctors were right.

Over the next two years, I was, in hospital terminology, a float nurse. When I reported for work I checked with the scheduling office. Wherever a nurse was needed that day is where they sent me. "Floating" afforded me a solid background of experience in nearly every department in the hospital—from the medical floor to neurology, urology, oncology, and the surgical floor. Occasionally I found myself working in the critical care units, which included the intensive care unit, the coronary care unit, and the emergency room.

At some point in the first two years a vague sense of dissatisfaction set in. One September morning I returned from a two-week vacation and something just wasn't right. Working on the surgical unit didn't give me a moment to think about it and when I got home in the afternoons I didn't want to think about it. I had been offered additional training by the nursing supervisors so I could work full-time in the critical care units and I had jumped at the chance. What was it about floor nursing that I was so eager to leave behind?

Working out on the floors, all three shifts around the clock, I was able to see many different aspects of life in the hospital. RNs were oftentimes accountable for up to twenty-five patients. Even with support staff (LPNs, nurses aides, and orderlies), rarely could I take the kind of time with patients that I wanted to. The days seemed to be filled up with giving medications, starting IVs, checking surgical sites, moving as quickly as possible from patient to patient, charting, handling paperwork, then starting that process over the next day. If a patient was having an especially hard time for whatever reason, I often sat with them after I was off duty. Only then could I give them my undivided attention and take the time to listen to them.

I chose nursing because I love people and I love life. Why was I feeling like an assembly-line worker in a completely impersonal environment?

So, the opportunity to be trained in critical care seemed perfect—one or two patients for each nurse. I knew I would have more time available for the patients and their families. No more assembly-line nursing for me or my patients. Did I ever have a lot to learn! Was I really that naive?

For the next month I was in classrooms from nine to five. There was so much more to learn. At the end of the four weeks, we were tested in every area. Having passed every test, from EKG readings to arterial lines, CVP (central venous pressure) lines, Swan Ganz catheters, many medications common to critical care patients, to the mechanics and workings of respirators, I was ready for the intensive care unit, coronary care unit, or the emergency room. I couldn't wait to get my assignment and was pleased that it was ICU—my home away from home for the next five years.

Although there were good times, even great times, a wonderful camaraderie with patients and their families, other nurses, medical students, interns, residents, doctors, lab techs, respiratory therapists, and unit secretaries, something was off for me. I had noticed it first in nursing school, then out on the regular floors in the hospital, and now it was occurring again in ICU. In diagnosing and treating patients, there seemed to be no connection made between the mind and body. It was as if the mind didn't exist, or was in no way related to the person who was the patient. The mind was entirely disregarded, and what we dealt with, and the only thing we dealt with for more than thirty seconds, was the body or symptom and treating those symptoms with surgery or drugs. I had a strong sense that patients were diminished by doctors and by the system. It was as if the patients were objects or things, to be fixed as quickly as possible by the doctors, not as fellow human beings and certainly not as partners.

In the intensive care unit, it was sometimes difficult to find the patients. They were completely surrounded by respirators, monitors for EKG, Swan Ganz and cardiac output readings, several IV lines, pumps for each IV line, extra lines for blood and plasma, urinary catheters, rectal tubes, chest tubes, drainage tubes, and bandages. Just imagine going into a hospital designed for people care and not being able to see people except through an entanglement of tubes, wires, lines, machinery, and high-tech blinking, noise-making apparatuses. I tried to imagine what it must be like for the patients and their families. I knew, as a nurse, I would have to become adept with all of the hardware quickly to be able to be with the person underneath all of that stuff.

I did accomplish that in a short time...and yet...

Why was there such a huge gap between what I had expected in being a nurse and what I found in our medical system? What was going on? It wasn't as if I were a brand new, twenty-two-year-old college graduate. I went back to complete nursing school, divorced, and became a single parent to my son, Peter. My state board results came in the mail three months before my thirtieth birthday. I had been active in my community, involved in local politics, and tuned into the concerns of our country at that time. I was well into the transition from an idealist to a hard-working, pragmatic single parent. None of these experiences, or years, could have prepared me for the shock I experienced as a registered nurse. I even remember wondering if there were something wrong with me in questioning the system instead of trusting my love for people, for life, and my own strong sense of self, decency, and basic, common sense.

For a long time I had wondered why I couldn't stay in nursing. Now I wonder how I lasted as long as I did.

Two

BEHIND THE SCENES: DANGEROUS

DOCTORS

Power undirected by a high purpose spells calamity.
                                        Theodore Roosevelt

*We never make mistakes. It's always the corpse's fault. And
the best of it is, dead men are very decent sort of folk. You
never hear them complain of the doctors who killed them.*
                                        Moliere
                        Dr. Sganarelle, Reluctant Doctor

I had been working as a registered nurse for just over five
years and had become a cog in a wheel of a giant machine,
never able to see the entire medical system for what it
was…until I took a leave of absence and traveled for several
months in cultures as different from ours as India, Thailand,
Australia, Egypt, Mexico, and Greece. Coming back into our
American culture, and more specifically, our medical culture,
there was an instant where I was able to see it from the outside
looking in, from a much broader perspective. The traveling
opened my eyes even wider and narrowed my tolerance for

American medicine's cut-and-drug addiction, and American medicine's addiction to fast, easy money.

For decades in this country, medicine has been held in high regard. After several years of study, mostly scientific study, doctors have enjoyed practicing medicine without restraints of any kind, accountable to no one, given a blind trust by citizens of this country. The majority of Americans still hold these beliefs of the godlike healing powers of doctors who they think have the answers. However, for those who have had friends and family suffer needless injuries or die at the hands of incompetent, or even worse, dangerous and egotistical doctors, know that the myth of American medical supremacy is often a lie. There are documented reports on millions of unnecessary surgeries, and millions of people taking billions of dollars' worth of prescription drugs for months and even years at a time, some of those drugs being worthless and even dangerous after a few days or weeks. There are also reports and statistics that indicate conventional American medicine cures less than ten percent of everyone and everything it tries to treat with surgery and drugs.

John Laster is a man I will never forget. He was admitted to ICU from the operating room after having one lung removed because of cancer. The cancer had metastasized (spread) so the respirator keeping John breathing was working overtime trying to get oxygen into the only lung he had left, which was full of cancer. Two of the three lobes were diseased. John was in his late sixties, physically small, lean, and tan. He had white hair, big blue eyes, and dimples I could see when he tried to smile around the tube that connected his lung to the respirator.

John and his wife, Emma, knew his diagnosis and prognosis (a prediction of the probable outcome of a disease), that the outcome was grim, and there was no cure for lung cancer. The surgery to remove his left lung might buy John a little more time. That was it. John and Emma had no children; the two of them had talked before his surgery and decided on no life support systems, if they became necessary to keep him alive after surgery. Shortly after meeting John, I had a brief conversation with Emma. While reading through John's chart before reporting on duty, I had seen the living will and wondered how he ended up in ICU, and how he and Emma felt about that. Emma seemed bewildered and told me Dr. Kaye had said John had not done well in surgery and had him brought to ICU and hooked him up to everything before she knew what was happening. Dr. Kaye had told her John had a chance of regaining strength and going home. He lied. I was assigned to John every day that I worked while he remained in ICU.

For a few days, John was coherent enough to communicate by writing short notes. I don't know why, but John and I hit it off; as a nurse, I quickly came to love the man. Within days of being admitted into ICU, John became angry, almost wild-eyed, at being in the unit, but his doctors were not listening to him, ignoring his and Emma's wishes. John was pretty philosophical about his life, his diagnosis, and his dying. He had come to accept the circumstances, and he was ready to move on.

John had two major insurance companies and was kept "alive" in ICU for almost six weeks—the last three incoherent and psychotic from the drugs, the monitors constantly beeping, lack of sleep, suctioning, and the tubes in every orifice of his body. During the first two weeks, John coded (cardiac arrested) several times. Twice, I was his nurse and, before calling the code, apologized and told him how sorry I was to be doing this to him, and that he and Emma were going to have to talk to Dr. Kaye again to stop the life support.

When a patient codes, that means either he has stopped breathing, or his heart has stopped or is in a rhythm that is ineffective and does not support life. Since John was on a respirator, which maintained his breathing (or respirations), each time he coded it was because his heart was giving out. Codes are last-ditch efforts to save someone's life. They are invasive and violent. Because of John's condition, his bones were brittle. By the second time we coded him, we cracked several of his ribs. As a result, every breath the respirator took for him was excruciatingly painful, even with IV valium and morphine given hourly.

I thought about John while driving home, on my days off, and driving back into the hospital. Sometimes I prayed he wouldn't make it through another code four. One morning I checked my assignment to see if John was still alive and went in to give him a hug before I took report. He had aged ten years in the two weeks he'd been in ICU. John was in four-point restraints. His arms and legs were tied to the sides of the bed. It brought an instant flood of tears to my eyes. He was put in restraints because he had pulled out his feeding tube and one of his IVs, his way of saying he had had enough of the hospital and the hardware. The doctors answer to that was to tie his arms and legs to the sides of the bed so he couldn't move, so that he had absolutely no control over his life or his death.

Glancing at the monitors and noticing a gray pallor to his skin, I walked in to the nurses' report room and said, "John's gonna code again soon, and I will not give him CPR again." A couple of the nurses looked shocked, but Alex, the nurse in charge, said, "I understand, Sydne. If John codes, page me and you can leave the room." Forty minutes later I hit the code button and called Alex. They revived John again, but even with the most powerful, potent drugs, John was barely hanging on and was beginning to lose it mentally. His outrage was palpable and even though I had only known John for a few weeks, I sensed that he had never in his life felt so helpless at being unable to stop all that was being done to him. Emma had spent most of each day in the ICU waiting room. She was allowed ten minutes per hour to be with John. This was standard hospital procedure. After thirty-nine years of marriage, Emma could spend approximately one hour and twenty minutes a day with her husband. She loved John, was afraid, and was becoming more and more exhausted herself.

I finally could no longer stand it. I followed his surgeon out of the room. I began to talk to Dr. Kaye, who kept walking and refused to look at me. I kept walking with him and talking to him. I wanted to know how many more times we were going to resuscitate John before we finally let him go. Dr. Kaye wheeled around, looked at me with rage in his eyes, and said coldly, "I have too much invested in him as his surgeon to let him die. I am going to get him home, even if he's only there for two minutes." Statistics were running the show again. Dr. Kaye had to show a certain success rate to keep operating, because he had been making so many mistakes in surgery. I also checked John's insurance companies and asked a friend in patient services to find out how much more eligibility John had. This information was not in the patients' charts, it was kept behind lock and key. Shirley got back to me with the information I wanted, and the day after the insurance companies stopped covering John, the doctors let him go. He died within minutes after being disconnected from all of the hardware.

On that day, and for days afterward, I wrestled with a lot of different emotions and thoughts and had questions that perhaps had no answers. As a nurse I was legally bound to follow doctors' orders. My job depended on it. Yet, I often disagreed with some of those orders. I also felt caught between patients and their families' wishes and what the doctors were ordering. It had become a moral dilemma for me. Were the doctors simply doing what they were trained to do, without thinking? Or had they struck a bargain with the hospital to keep the beds full? Was there an underlying agenda the patients, their families, and the nurses were not aware of?

I began to talk with and question other nurses I worked alongside of in ICU. Some of them had already sensed my dilemma and offered advice and whatever support they could. While there were a few who I could say completely agreed with my sense of things, what I found was that many of the nurses were willing to follow doctors' orders and just do their job. Others were open enough to tell me that they had long ago given up trying to make any changes. They were just going to show up for work, do their job, and get by until they could retire. The one issue we agreed on unanimously was that nurses were not given a powerful voice in their roles as professional care givers and patient advocates. Another way to say that is to say nurses were there to follow doctors' orders, period, even though nurses spent hours with the patients while doctors spent moments or minutes. It sounded too much to me like unthinking, robotic behavior. I was left asking myself, "For this I needed college?" I was also saddened by these women who had started out with a vision and enthusiasm about what was possible in health care in making a contribution with their careers, and who had been reduced to waiting to retire. They were mired in their resignation and not about to step out again. They had given up. I wondered how many horrible incidents and years it had taken them to get to that point, while reassuring myself that it would never happen to me. But even as I reassured myself, I felt my own suspicion; I no longer trusted the medical system to take care of people. I began to pay closer attention to all the patients and doctors in ICU, not just the patients to whom I was assigned. And I began to take notes.

One morning, Ronnie, the head nurse in the coronary care unit (CCU), was talking to me at the nurses' station in ICU. The CCU was empty, but she needed to stay "in house" in case of any admissions. Within minutes, the chief of staff of CCU walked by, stopped to say hello, and said to Ronnie, "We're not making any money with CCU empty; I'll have it filled up by three PM." He did. I called Ronnie after reporting off in ICU, and all eight beds were filled. The next morning I arrived a few minutes early to check out a hunch. I walked into CCU, flipped open each chart to the back, and found what I was looking for. Every single patient had at least one major insurance company. Good thing, since just being wheeled through the doors of CCU cost about forty-five hundred dollars. I called Ronnie at home that night, and my worst suspicions were confirmed. She couldn't figure out why any of the eight patients were in CCU. They didn't need to be there, but the hospital and doctors needed them and their insurance companies to be there—they needed to make money.

The medical system and the whole medical industry is, in some basic ways, like any other corporation or business venture. Those with the most at stake (read money here) will do whatever it takes to win, to succeed, to look good, to be right, and to justify their behavior and actions, whatever they are. This behavior may be implicit in being human; it is automatic and unthinking. But at some level, every one of us knows when there has been a lapse of integrity. The automatic next move is to enroll others in the justifications and to get agreement for whatever actions have been taken. In this way, people are enrolled as accomplices to the original crime. Decency and fairness are no longer driving the words and actions and neither is a professional oath of honor or the hospital's mission statement. This, in part, accounts for business as usual, maintaining the status quo, and a conspiracy of mediocrity and silence, keeping things just the way they are and the way they have "always" been. I began to see that doctors were serving themselves and the institutions of medicine, not the patients. Under these circumstances, very few people would dare to rock the boat. Those that do are labeled troublemakers or crackpots and are made to feel there is something wrong with them, not the system.

Al Jensen was a man in his mid-sixties. He had been diagnosed with diabetes nearly thirty years earlier. Diabetes interferes with the circulatory system, and the first place to see the effects are the extremities: legs, feet, arms, and hands. He was back in ICU because the gangrene that had caused first his feet, then his legs below the knees, then his legs above the knees to be amputated had spread up into his groin and scrotum. It was a strange case. How much more of this man were the surgeons going to amputate? He was still able to breath on his own, but was on powerful, very expensive drugs in an effort to keep his heart beating in a regular pattern. As far as we could tell, he was completely terrified. The doctors were keeping him hopeful, while he watched the gangrene spread into his penis and abdomen. He ended up on a respirator, no longer able to breath on his own. We were able to keep him "alive" for another three weeks—completely mentally disoriented. The last ten days of his life, he didn't even recognize his wife.

Gail was a darling—funny and smart. She was married, had two preteenage children, and taught fifth and sixth graders. I made it a point to talk to Sharon, the nurse who had admitted Gail into the hospital. Sharon told me Gail was bright, energetic, enthusiastic, and had a huge zest and love for life. Gail loved teaching school, and it showed. She had recently been chosen teacher of the year. Gail told Sharon she had been teaching for eight years and had a powerful vision for the possibility of education and the difference it could make in this country. Gail said she had always been the "picture of health," except for her hiatal hernia, which she found annoying because it began to interfere with her busy schedule; it was clear that this woman was someone who impacted thousands of people. She had flown up from California to have a simple procedure (invented and perfected in the Northwest) to repair a hiatal hernia. I didn't take care of her because she never made it out to the surgical floor, let alone into ICU. Sharon, who worked on the surgical floor and who had admitted Gail, came down to let me know about the latest Dr. Lukas fiasco. Dr. Lukas inadvertently nicked Gail's aorta. She bled to death on the operating table.

Late one afternoon I got a call from the nursing office. Though I had just gotten home from work, I was asked to come back in and take care of a brain surgery patient. Nancy had just gone into surgery, so I wouldn't need to be there until 9:30 PM. I said yes, headed for the shower, checked to make sure I had a clean uniform, and put on a pot of coffee. It would be twenty-four hours without sleep, but I'd done it before and lived. Besides, as usual, we were short-staffed in ICU and everyone was on the ragged edge. I arrived in ICU by 9:15 and got the room set up.

I kept an eye on the double-door entrance of ICU and began helping other nurses with their patients. By eleven o'clock, I was getting anxious. Had Nancy coded in the OR? Were there complications? Was she still alive? Finally, I called over to the OR. Nancy was still in surgery, predicted time of arrival in ICU was now 12:30 AM. I wondered what, if anything, had happened.

At 1:10 the phone at the nurses' station rang; thirty seconds later the double doors banged opened. The resident looked at me, asked, "Who is taking care of this patient?" and groaned when I said, "I am." He told me to keep my mouth shut and just take the report from the neurosurgeon, that he would come back and talk to me privately. As Dan finished saying that, I'm sure my eyes were as big as saucers, because he smiled and shook his head. In moments I was surrounded by the attending physicians, resident, interns, a respiratory therapist, and an anesthesiologist.

Nancy had brain surgery for a tumor on the right side of her head. I was more than curious to find out what else had happened. I quietly and calmly took the report from the neurosurgeon as I got all the lines and monitors hooked up and rechecked every reading for accuracy. Nancy was still completely under the effects of the anesthesia, deep in sleep and completely unresponsive. My only tip-off was that is was a bitemporal craniotomy, which indicated both sides of the brain were involved in the surgery. As soon as we got the patient settled in, everything hooked up and connected, and everyone out of the room, I looked at Dan and said, "Okay, what happened in there that no one's talking about?" Dan put a hand on my shoulder, as if to calm or restrain me. He said slowly, "Sydne, we couldn't find the tumor; we were four hours into the surgery and even double-checked to make sure we had the right patient. We couldn't figure out what was going on. We finally realized we had been working on the wrong side of the brain. The x-ray had been hung up backwards. So, we sewed up one side, started on the other, found the tumor, got it, and the patient has a chance of recovering.

Or, she may end up with scrambled eggs for brains. In any event, the patient and her family will never know what happened."

The first question to go through my mind was, "Is there anyone who cares about this patient and her family?" then, "Who are we here to take care of?" With Dan telling me to keep my mouth shut, and my keeping my mouth shut, another enrollment to conspire to protect doctors and hospitals had just occurred. Dan was one of the residents I respected the most. The neurosurgeon was another doctor I had utmost respect for. He had made a mistake. Why was the automatic next move to cover it up? Do we expect doctors to be perfect? Do they expect perfection from themselves—so much so that when a mistake occurs it cannot even be spoken of? What happens to all those who look the other way, from the whole team of health care providers to hospital administration? I felt diminished, discouraged, upset, and sad. My estimation of Dan and the neurosurgeon plummeted, not just because of the mistake, but because it became another mistake immediately covered up, with no one taking accountability.

Especially after this incident, I began to notice our whole health care team's determination to look good at any cost, to protect themselves and survive, and to continue to try to live up to their carefully nurtured, godlike public image. What if doctors began admitting mistakes, admitting that sometimes they didn't have the answers, and began to communicate with the rest of their health care team, patients, and patients' families, sharing their own disappointments and failures, and treating other human beings as equals? Perhaps doctors' dreaded fear of medical malpractice would dissipate and even disappear.

Dr. Routh was a disaster. His reputation among nurses in ICU preceded him; I had been warned about him days before I met him. He continually made mistakes in surgery and the ICU nurses felt his patients were lucky to be alive after he got hold of them. One day I had the chance to meet and work with him. He had done thoracic surgery on Brian, a man in his mid-forties, and Brian wasn't doing well. A chest tube had to be put into Brian's lung to drain off excess fluid. I got the chest pack from central supply and got the room set up for the procedure. Dr. Routh came in, noticed everything was ready to go, and broke open the chest pack. Less than a minute into the procedure, I got scared. Dr. Routh was shaking so badly I didn't know if he was going through withdrawal from alcohol or if he had just tanked up on cocaine or had Parkinson's disease. I remember looking around for help, anyone to interrupt the procedure for a moment. No one was there so in desperation I intentionally contaminated the sterile field by picking up a tube lying on the patient's chest before I put sterile gloves on. It looked like a stupid mistake, but I didn't care. I knew I would have to order a new chest pack setup from central supply, and that it would buy me a few minutes out of the room.

Denise, who was an excellent nurse, clinically, as well as loving and compassionate with patients and staff, had been watching me through the window. As I came running out of the room I ran into her; she was doubled over laughing. She said she had been waiting to see my reaction to Dr. Routh, and between my contaminating the field and my eyes being wide as saucers, she wasn't disappointed. I was so upset, I grabbed her, and with her face two inches from mine, said, "Can Dr. Routh get this tube into the patient, or is it going to end up in the wall behind us? Why is he shaking so badly? Is he always like this? Is he on drugs?" Denise was still laughing at my reaction, but did say he would probably be able to do the procedure. The chest tube placement was successful, but I was outraged. Later, I found out Dr. Routh's shaking, or palsy, was explained away as a part of his aging. He continued to shake and continued to do surgery. Apparently, no one was willing to address the problems of a shaky surgeon. This patient's life, as well as many other patients' lives, were at risk because of this doctor's ego. There didn't seem to be any way to stop him.

Kyle was a beautiful young man with red hair, freckles, bright blue eyes, and a big grin. He was married to Lori and was the father of two young boys. If ever a family fit my image of an ideal family, this was it. It was so apparent that Kyle and Lori were in love and happy, we all felt like we were intruding into private, intimate space when we needed to go into his room to change his bandages or give him medication.

Kyle was an architect, loved his work, and was also an avid sportsman, who loved hunting and fishing and was anxious to teach his sons, Drew and David, everything he knew about the outdoors. The boys were as cute as their parents. Even in the hospital setting, the boys could not contain their curiosity and energy or their love for their mom and dad.

I got the opportunity to talk to Kyle a lot because I took care of him in ICU. He should never have ended up in ICU, but the surgeon's hand had slipped, and, rather than performing just the scheduled appendectomy, he cut Kyle's diaphragm by mistake and failed to notice that for several minutes. Kyle was now faced with hyperbaric treatments and eventually the onset of gangrene in his legs, which led to the loss of his legs. As far as I know, he never questioned that it could have been the doctor's fault. Of course the doctor never told him, either. A young man's life, and the lives of Lori, Drew, and David, had been changed forever. The doctor acted as if nothing out of the ordinary had happened—just another day in the life of a doctor and one of his many patients.

Kyle's story is just one example of an opportunity for the whole health care team to pull together and debrief on what worked and what didn't work, and to make some sense of it by training and developing a powerful team and by telling the truth. This was an opportunity to communicate and work together, to support each other, to be in communication with Kyle and Lori in a meaningful way to look at possibilities and, somehow, to take accountability for the mistakes that are made. Instead, Kyle and Lori's experience became just one more cover-up.

Can you imagine a carpenter or building contractor not

being in communication with the architect about the integrity of the house or office building they worked on together? What if a major structural beam was left out before an area was dry-walled in? Would they continue to build the structure and hope it stands without the beam? Or what if a teacher decided to keep quiet about a major incident that happened in the classroom and swore the class to secrecy, even keeping the incident from the parents and principal? In most professions this kind of cover-up is not tolerated. There are checks and balances in place to maintain some kind of integrity. Not so in health care. Cover-ups are the norm.

On a national newscast last week we were told if we were scheduled for surgery, it would be a good idea for us to mark our surgical site with a marking pen to make sure the surgery was performed in the correct place; if an extremity was involved to mark the arm or leg to be operated on, and to mark the other extremity with NOT THIS ONE.

One of the most bizarre cases involved a doctor named Gary Brendan. Struggling to build up a successful practice, he got impatient and started taking patients out of nursing homes and performing unnecessary surgeries on them. When we realized what was going on, we were horrified. Several other nurses and myself began talking to nursing supervisors and even a few of the doctors we trusted. This man's life was about making a lot of money, at any cost. Dr. Brendan's drive to make money had nothing whatsoever to do with a successful, satisfying medical practice. His colleagues all continued to turn the other way. No one seemed willing or able to take any definitive or immediate action. It was almost four years and hundreds of patients later that Dr. Brendan finally lost his license in this state. He moved to another state and continues to practice medicine.

Dr. Sean Burt, once an excellent surgeon, had been strung out on cocaine and who knows what other drugs for months. He had installed a water bed in one of the back offices in his clinic, and his life had become about sex, drugs, and rock and roll. He certainly had the right to do that, except he still possessed a medical license and was performing surgeries on people who had trusted him with their lives *while* he was under the influence. Though it was tragic that none of his friends could get him off the drugs, even more tragic were the mistakes he was making in surgery. No one was ever able to stop him until he stopped himself. He, and one of his girlfriends, overdosed on a combination of drugs and alcohol in a local hotel.

Why had Sean turned to drugs? At this point, all that anyone could say would be conjecture. He seemed like a great guy, but did any one of us really know him? Why didn't one of his colleagues, or a hospital administrator, step in and provide some kind of support for this highly trained and highly skilled man? Didn't anyone care? Didn't anyone think they could make a difference with him? Were we all too busy with our own lives, or were we unwilling to confront our own, automatic, human-being apathy? Was being a doctor and surgeon a big disappointment for Sean? Did he, on some level, feel he had sold his soul, compromised his ideals? Did he really feel it was acceptable to cut into people while on cocaine? We will never know.

One afternoon I walked in to do a physical assessment on a patient who had recently come back from open-heart surgery. A medical resident, Andy Wheeler, a sweet, dedicated young man from the Midwest, was injecting my patient's morphine into a heparin lock (portable IV) he had put into his own arm.

Dr. Aaron Phillips, an orthopedic surgeon, kept making mistakes in the operating room. He was so bad the hospital wouldn't let him perform surgery without another surgeon being in the operating room with him. He even scared other doctors who kept hearing about him. He was a topic of conversation all over the hospital. Actually, he was a topic of gossip. I don't know if anyone ever spoke with him about getting retrained or brushing up on skills he was lacking. I do know that everyone made fun of him, while lives were being lost. At a special meeting with ICU nurses, we were told the hospital was finally suspending his surgical privileges and had recommended that he have a psychiatric evaluation. He lost his surgical privileges at one hospital in the city, moved to a small town in southern Washington, and was welcomed by the local hospital, heralded by the community who felt they were fortunate to be getting a big-city doctor.

Even if Aaron had wanted to improve his surgical performance, what was in place in the hospital to support that? Perhaps with the pervasive, undermining gossip, he didn't have a chance of ever getting any better. Medicine and hospitals are not organized for dealing with doctors' incompetence, lack of training, or even lack of confidence. There was no cracking down on doctors making mistakes; there was no place to go with concerns or complaints.

Why is it, in a hospital setting, it takes years to expose and deal with dangerous doctors? How is the medical profession set up that an incompetent doctor can continue to practice for years in the same hospital or simply move to another hospital, another town, or another state and continue practicing dangerous medicine? This is about more than dangerous medicine; it is about people being killed by doctors they trust.

One afternoon I was in a patient's room, calibrating all the monitors, when the surgical resident, Bruce Nelson, stopped by to check on his patient. We had had some great conversations over the past few months during his rotation through ICU. We even agreed that some of the patients we were coding should have been allowed to die with some dignity, surrounded by their families instead of all the technology and machines. I noticed Bruce looked pale and his eyes were bloodshot. I said, "Bruce, were you on call last night?" He turned around and said in a cold, harsh voice, "I prefer to be called Dr. Nelson." It so surprised me, I burst out laughing and told him he was about twenty years too late, that nurses were not even required to stand when a doctor entered the room. Then I asked him what was really going on. He sat down in the chair by the patient's bed and said, "Sydne, I hate medicine. I hate the direction it's going, I hate what we do to people, I hate hospitals." He looked like he was fifty years old. He was twenty-six. I asked him what he would like to do, if he could do anything, and how he ended up in medical school. He said what he really loved was snow skiing; he had wanted to be a ski instructor, but his father had insisted he carry on the family tradition of being a doctor. Before he left he added that he owed his parents too much money to even consider changing careers, that it was too late for him. I wondered how many other doctors, like Bruce, hated what they were doing, but felt trapped by the years of study, their families' expectations, as well as their own expectations of themselves and the financial debts they faced.

On an even broader scale, the entire anesthesiology department in a large, suburban hospital was finally put under review because over a period of eighteen months there had been a brain-death rate (resulting in comas) three times higher than the national average. One of the most horrible things about this was that it made for great conversation within the medical community, but was never made public, never published in a local newspaper. We did hear that the anesthesiologists were reading books, taking bathroom breaks, smoke breaks, and making phone calls while patients were under general anesthesia. One of the anesthesiologists was required to see a psychiatrist for therapy; the others didn't even get their hands slapped. Meanwhile, the patients and their families had no idea what was going on. The anesthesiologist required to see a psychiatrist had given my best friend an epidural just before her son was born, several months earlier. It made my skin crawl to think of that. Another doctor at that hospital, who happened to be a friend of mine, attempted to justify the latest fiasco by saying anesthesiologists had a very boring job, which is why they were so highly paid, and why they had been taking breaks while they had patients under general anesthesia.

American medicine has produced surgery addicts. The following cases are just two of many examples.

One of the more macabre things I witnessed occurred one morning when a man named Gordon Jacobsen wanted to show me his scars from previous surgeries as I was getting him ready for his abdominal surgery, scheduled for the next day. This man was ecstatic, describing his eight previous major surgeries to me, wanting me to see every scar, as if they were war wounds he had earned.

Within days, I went in to get a woman ready for surgery, and she had been up for hours, fixing her hair, her nails, her makeup, as if she were preparing for a stage debut, which in her mind, she was. She told me it was her fourteenth surgery— a fact she seemed very proud of.

Can it really be this bad? It's much worse than anything I've been able to portray. And it happens day after day in every hospital and health care facility across the country.

You may be thinking, "Not my doctor, not my hospital, not in my town," but how do you know? If I hadn't worked inside the health-care system, I wouldn't have believed it either. It's tough to confront that you may have been deceived and defrauded by your own doctor and your local hospital, by people you trusted. This blind trust is part of what keeps the system in place. Rather than confront the possibility that the medical system has victimized you, it's easier to ignore it, deny it, or hope that it hasn't happened to you, or it doesn't happen in your town. The doctors and hospitals understand this reasoning. In fact, they count on it. There are saints and sinners in every profession. Doctors are people too, but they have been given an inordinate amount of trust by the American public, or, maybe more correctly, they have sold us on trusting them. They have even created a power, of sorts, over us with their arrogance. Who would dare question a doctor's

diagnosis? But not only have doctors and hospitals betrayed
our trust, they have, along with the drug and insurance
companies and the medical equipment and supply companies,
caused enormous damage and suffering to millions of people
and abused their power for decades. There is no way to
account for the millions of unnecessary surgeries and the
millions of people on the continued use of unnecessary prescription drugs.

I kept denying this, even to myself. I kept thinking it
couldn't be this bad. I even worked for a few months at two
other local hospitals, hoping to see a difference. The only
difference I found was that the other two hospitals were worse.
Whenever I brought this up with doctors who knew me and
were friends, there were no answers and no hope of it ever
getting any better. At best, what they said was that it (medicine) had always been that way and probably always would be.
After all, it was called the *practice* of medicine. This was
sometimes followed by laughter. The doctors who laughed
were passively aiding and abetting every incompetent, dangerous doctor in their own hospital and in every health care
facility across the country. I couldn't find anyone willing to
take a stand for it ever being any better or even different.
Unable and unwilling to compromise my vision for what
could be and my own basic sense of integrity any longer, and
finding it increasingly more difficult to face myself, I left the
medical field and knew I would not work within that system
again.

As I watch our government struggle with health care
reform issues, I am captivated by the doctors defending
themselves, defending the medical system, defending their
salaries, defending the millions of unnecessary surgeries they
perform every year, defending the medical schools' archaic
teaching methods, defending the billions of dollars of drugs
they prescribe every year, just plain defending everything the
way that it is. Add to the doctors the AMA, insurance and drug
companies, special interest groups, political action committees,
also known as lobbyists, who buy off our elected officials.

They have gone on the offensive, advertising like never before the wonderful benefits of American medicine—the best in the world.

The con they've been running on the American public for decades is just beginning to be exposed. And they are angry and defensive only because it will mean a loss of revenue for them—a decline in their perceived power and prestige—not because of any altruistic sentiments.

The AMA is advertising itself and its "services" like never before—on television, radio, billboards, and in magazines. They have even added toll-free numbers for us to call them, so we can hear their propaganda, personally, and for free.

In the meantime, medicine as it is practiced today is spending our children's and our grandchildren's money. Billions of dollars are spent every year to support American medicine as it is practiced today. The cost of the American medical system is fast approaching one and a half trillion dollars a year. The cost now is almost twenty percent of the gross national product. Western Europe, which has a medical system that covers everyone, spends eight percent of their GNP. What makes these numbers even more bizarre is that American medicine rarely cures anything; it merely masks the symptoms. We now have a medical bureaucracy that operates for its own benefit and survival, spending millions of dollars a year on their public image. The medical industry has enough money to have a separate industry just to defend itself and promote its public image. In other words, the medical industry has enough money to justify everything it has done and continues to do. It is right and we are wrong. Who could possibly know better than they do what is best for all the rest of us? And how could we dare to question them? This is nothing more than mass propaganda designed to keep doctors and the medical industry in what they perceive as their rightful position of power.

I only know of a few doctors who have publicly told the truth about what's going on today in the health-care system. A couple of them have written excellent, straightforward books on the subject of our national disgrace. Obviously, it's not enough.

Culturally, we are still taught to trust the medical system and doctors. We have trusted doctors and American medicine, and we have all been burned, if only in our pocketbooks. Over time, this trust becomes tinged with skepticism, then finally cynicism. "If you can't trust your doctor, who can you trust?" is a cultural adage, but a faulty one.

I have a friend named Mary who was a registered nurse but went back to law school and is now a medical malpractice attorney. She has to deal with the doctors who finally make enough mistakes, or blatant enough mistakes, and are held accountable for them by patients who have the courage to take them to court. She says, "It's been my experience as a nurse, and a malpractice attorney, that there are a lot of doctors who do not care at all about their patients. They're in medicine for the money, the power, and the prestige, and they are outraged that anyone dares to question them, even when they've made the most horrible mistakes, including causing death. The medical profession has gone unmonitored by anyone for so long, it has become dangerous."

It seems that only people outside of the medical system can see some of the absurdities and the danger. A few nurses' voices are not going to be enough to effect any kind of change, let alone any kind of transformation of this dangerous, unmonitored system. It is going to take every single one of us.

To alter culture, especially our American medical culture, which at this point in time is entrenched and ingrained in our minds and thinking, in the media and advertising, would be a historical event. It is time for such an event. And it will take all of us waking up to the lies of doctors and the American medical industry and demanding excellence—and genuine caring and compassion from this system. It is time to stop the cut-and-drug addiction that we have all been supporting.

I've speculated on what would happen if hospital administrations were required by law to report every mistake made in the hospitals and the results were published once a week in a local newspaper, hospital by hospital, doctor by doctor. How about doctors being required, by law, to let their patients know of any past or pending malpractice litigation they are involved in, or have been involved in, simply as a way of protecting the potential patient? How about doctors who make repeated mistakes being sent back to a retraining program? How about programs like this being set up in medical schools now, not twenty years from now? How about doctors and hospital administrators being held accountable for the incompetent, dangerous doctors around them, in their hospitals, and in their communities? How about setting up review boards for statistical results on every single doctor practicing medicine in this country? Why have doctors and hospitals gotten away with so much for so long?

A partial solution and a place to start would be for each of us to be accountable for our health, our bodies, and our well-being, and to question everything doctors do. I think it would change the face of American medicine. It might even change doctors' attitudes. Why isn't this done? Why don't we begin demanding it? Why are our lives put at stake because of doctors' egos?

Let's publicly identify the lobbyists and the special interest groups. Who are they? Where are they? Who pays them? How much do they make? Who do they answer to? Who are they accountable to? Why are they kept behind the scenes? How much are they spending to lobby our elected officials in Congress? Who has received money from them? And how much money have they taken? What are they protecting? What have they got to hide? The politics behind medicine may be worse than the practice of medicine itself.

Since very little is being done within the medical system to protect us from dangerous doctors and unnecessary procedures, drugs, and surgeries, we must begin to protect ourselves, instead of continuing to protect doctors, hospitals, the drug and insurance companies, medical schools, the medical equipment and supply companies, medical laboratories, and a wildly out-of-control, dysfunctional medical system. The health, or better said, the disease and disaster, industry have created and supported huge constituencies in business: the media, advertising companies, government, FDA, AMA, drug and insurance companies, and special interest groups and lobbyists bought off or at least in collusion with the medical industry. These factions could all be characterized as parasitic. They are feeding off of us and each other for money. Their existence has nothing to do with our health. They continue, in part, because of all the propaganda they have given us over the years, advertising in every form of media that we need them.

We do not need them, they need us, and they need for there to be something wrong with us that only they can remedy.

Three

NO DEATHS ALLOWED: HIGH-TECH

BARBARIANISM

Death is not the greatest loss in life. The greatest loss is what dies within us while we live.

Norman Cousins

Keeping patients alive has become an enormous money-making business, an integral part of keeping hospitals and doctors afloat financially. Much of American medicine has become about high drama, rescue medicine, and doctors as heroes—very expensive in dollars as well as suffering by people caught up as hostages in hospitals that have very little compassion and respect for human beings unless they have at least one, if not two, insurance companies to cover their bills. I'm not referring to the average person going in for an average surgery, if there is such a thing as an average surgery. I am referring to elderly people coming to the natural end of their lives, or people with cancer that has metastasized all over the body, people with no lung capacity left—in short, people with acute, terminal prognoses.

I have seen living wills ignored time after time. At first I was shocked, but it is standard operating procedure. It is a cold, hard fact that if you are covered by an insurance company—better yet, two insurance companies—you will be on life support systems until your insurance runs out—living will or not. Ask any nurse; she or he will tell you—once you are a patient in any hospital, you have no rights. Once you are a patient in a hospital, you are a number in a bed, with insurance coverage—a major source of revenue for the medical industry.

The medical community is not entirely to blame for this phenomena. Over the past three or four decades, medicine has made great strides technologically. We have come to expect miracle drugs and miracle cures. We have also become addicted to fast, easy answers, and fast, easy cures; one pill for this symptom, surgery for another symptom—in other words, anything the doctors want to do and what they are trained to do.

This brings in the pharmaceutical (from this point on referred to as drug) companies. The major drug companies have become accustomed to their multibillion-dollar businesses and they will do whatever it takes to stay in business and keep their profit margins up, which means keeping you on drugs. One result of this phenomena is that over-medication is the leading health hazard among the elderly. Every single synthetic drug has side effects. Rarely do doctors let people know of possible or probable side effects. I have seen doctors tell patients to ask their pharmacists, but the days of the neighborhood drugstore and the possibility of a friendship or even being known by your pharmacist is disappearing fast, if it is not already completely gone. So who answers questions people may have about the medications being prescribed for them? No one. And yet, as a culture, we take more pills per capita than any other nation on earth. Alternatives to synthetic drugs are not an option the drug companies are going to tolerate.

Add to this the medical equipment companies and the

medical supply companies, along with the insurance companies that are making millions of dollars off of your symptoms, and you can begin to get a sense of the conspiracy to have person after person admitted to hospitals and treated. These companies wouldn't call it a conspiracy, but what else is it? After all, these companies want to stay in business and keep making their huge profits. There is a great deal invested in this country in us not being healthy, in us being at the beck and call of doctors, hospitals, medical laboratories, drug companies, insurance companies, and medical supply and equipment companies. They need you, or rather they need your body, your money, and your insurance coverage.

Always, under the auspices of humanitarian reasons, "life" is prolonged in the hospital. Too many companies, and people, have too much invested to do otherwise. And most of them will completely justify it in the name of medicine and humanity.

Add to this the media, show business, New York, and Hollywood. They have given us Ben Casey, M.D., Dr. Kildare, *Marcus Welby, M.D., Rescue 911, General Hospital, Emergency, M.A.S.H., The Doctors, Chicago Hope, ER,* and *St. Elsewhere*, just to name a few. These shows and movies, along with all the commercials with doctors' recommendations, have been promoted and sold to us, covertly shaping our thinking, or better said, our unthinking and acceptance of "modern medicine" and doctors' portrayal not only as heroes, but as the only course of possible action for responsible people.

Over time we have also been trained to not trust ourselves, but to trust our doctors. Doctors take advantage of this. To the medical system, death equals failure. Medicine has become about extending life, at all costs, no matter the quality of that life or the patients' wishes. Never mind that someone is ninety-three years old and in renal failure, or seventy-nine years old with a heart about ready to give out, or fifty-four years old and completely filled with cancer. Doctors are now trained to keep you alive so you can spend the last few days or weeks of your life on life-support machinery in your local intensive care unit. Why die at home when you, and your insurance companies, can spend thousands and thousands of dollars to have you die slowly, over time, in your local ICU?

If you don't think we're a death-denying culture, look for yourself. We're surrounded by advertising done mostly with young people. Many of the top models are in their teens. The cosmetic industry is having a heyday with their antiaging formulas and wrinkle-reducing creams. All kinds of hair-care formulas to cover gray hair are on the market. Plastic surgery is the fastest-growing specialty in medicine, and in this area, we are barraged by commercials on television, radio, and in newspapers, selling their magic.

On a more serious note, do you have a will made out? Do you have a living will, if you're not interested in being kept alive on life-support machinery? Have you discussed your death and burial arrangements with your partner, family, doctor, or clergy, or even seriously thought about it for yourself? We don't talk about it or plan for it. We ignore death and live like we have forever or we pretend death only happens to other people. You're not the only one. Many doctors haven't faced their own mortality, or made any of these arrangements for themselves (which may, in part, be why so many of them ignore living wills and DNR (do not resuscitate) orders. By not dealing with death as a natural end to life, we support doctors and their training in a system where death is the enemy, to be avoided at all costs.

While I was working in ICU, prolonging life became a bad joke among nurses and a few doctors. The only solution we could come up with was to have DNR (do not resuscitate) or no-code (no life support) tattooed on our chests. Every one of us knew we would never go through what the majority of our ICU patients went through. Though we joked about it, we were serious about it. The power of doctors, in this kind of situation, scared all of us. It scared us because there was no stopping the doctors from hooking up every patient to every piece of life-support machinery available and starting, and keeping, patients on powerful, expensive drugs and respirators, no matter what the prognosis.

I've spoken to many people who are afraid of death. The best thing I could tell them was to go observe in any ICU for two or three days, then come back and tell me whether they were scared of dying, or scared of being kept alive.

Gloria, a seventy-six-year-old great-grandmother, was admitted to ICU. Her original diagnosis was ovarian cancer. However, within a few months, despite radiation treatment and chemotherapy, the cancer had metastasized everywhere. Her body was filled with cancer, from the lymph nodes to her lungs, pelvis, and had just entered her brain. Why was she in ICU? We had no miracle cures there among the hardware. I read the doctors' orders, in the front of the chart, in total disbelief. She was to be hooked up to every piece of life-support machinery known to man, including a respirator to keep her breathing. What we were doing to her was cruel. Gloria was incoherent. Her family was confused; they didn't know what to do. I talked and listened to them; what I heard amazed me. The doctor still had hope and had recommended everything be done to keep her alive. I flipped to the back of the chart and found what I was looking for—two insurance companies, which meant every little thing, and not so little thing, would be done to her to keep her alive. Dr. Abrams, I thought, must be a new doctor, just setting up his practice, and in dire need of making a lot of money fast. Personally, and as a professional R.N., I could not reconcile this woman being a patient in ICU. Gloria spent her last few weeks on this earth completely mentally disoriented and in ICU. Dr. Abrams and the hospital made a lot of money.

Floyd was a seventy-one-year-old man, admitted into ICU after open-heart surgery. Floyd was not doing well, and in reading through his physical and history in his chart, I was stunned that Dr. Brad Dillon had performed open-heart surgery on this patient. He had an interstitial lung disease for which there is no cure and no definitive treatment. He had also been suffering from short-term memory loss for the previous two and a half to three years. Senile dementia and Alzheimer's disease were possibilities. He came out of the anesthetic confused and disoriented; there was talk among the doctors that he had suffered a "neuro event" during the surgery. He didn't recognize his wife or their children. His condition continued to deteriorate; meanwhile, his primary doctor, Dr. Dillon, had gone on vacation

One morning, Floyd's wife, Arlene, asked to talk to Pat, the nurse taking care of her husband. She told Pat that she and her children had discussed Floyd's care, and, given his deteriorating condition and mental status, they wanted Floyd taken off all life-support drugs, machines, and equipment. The children, Steven, Marsha, and Kelly, all in their thirties and early forties, agreed that their father would not want to be kept alive mechanically. Pat called Dr. Gail Sawyer, who was covering for Dr. Dillon. Dr. Sawyer came in later that day; Arlene and her kids had waited to see her. After talking to them, Dr. Sawyer informed them that while she was responsible for Dr. Dillon's patients, she would not write the no-code order needed to stop the life support. Upset, Arlene came out to the nurses' station and asked us to call Dr. Peterson, the pulmonary (lung) specialist who was involved in Floyd's care. He, too, refused to write the order.

Several issues were involved here. The first was that both Dr. Sawyer and Dr. Peterson refused accountability and responsibility for Floyd and his family's wishes. They both simply chose to ignore the family's decision, which was arrived at after much deliberation, discussion, and soul searching. For a family to choose to withdraw life support can be an agonizing decision to come to. Even though Arlene, Steven, Marsha, and Kelly requested, then demanded the doctors withdraw life support, the doctors continued their own agenda, which was keeping Floyd alive. Drs. Sawyer and Peterson had the authority to stop all life support. They chose not to.

The second issue was the lack of courage by Dr. Sawyer

and Dr. Peterson despite the courage demonstrated by Floyd's family. The nursing staff watched these two doctors actively try to avoid seeing the family members over the next few days. We saw them step into other patients' rooms, as well as the nurses' lounge, in order to not come face to face with the family. I don't know if they were simply cowards or ashamed of their actions or inaction.

The third issue was that Floyd's condition continued to deteriorate, physiologically and psychologically. Floyd was incoherent and going downhill fast. The family could do nothing but stand by and watch it happen, all of them knowing Floyd would not have wanted it that way.

After requesting life support be stopped, and Drs. Sawyer and Peterson refusing, Floyd was kept alive for another ten days—until Dr. Dillon returned from vacation. So the last memories for Arlene of her husband, and the last memories for Steven, Marsha, and Kelly of their father is of Floyd being on powerful IV drugs to maintain his heartbeat and blood pressure, a respirator breathing for him, IVs, a urinary catheter, an EKG monitor and Swan Ganz line tracing Floyd's irregular heartbeat, and powerful, tranquilizing medications to calm his increasing agitation. Lloyd and his family suffered needlessly for nine more days because the doctors either didn't listen, chose not to respond, or both. Any one of these doctors could have written the no-code order, or they could have called Dr. Dillon and interrupted his vacation for five minutes. They didn't do either.

Last, but not least, Floyd's extra nine days in ICU amounted to somewhere between twenty thousand and thirty thousand dollars. Interesting to note, Floyd had insurance coverage as well as Medicare.

When Dr. Dillon returned from vacation, he spoke to the family and immediately stopped all life support. Floyd died peacefully and quietly within minutes.

Jack was a big, handsome teddy bear of a man in his late fifties. He ended up my patient in ICU after a major stroke. His wife Claren was in shock. She and Jack had played eighteen holes of golf the day before and gone out to dinner with friends the night before. Jack stepped out of the shower on a Sunday morning, collapsed, and never regained consciousness. Their children, Susan and Jennifer, were coming out of shock when I met them and had begun grieving for their father. Jack, at fifty-eight years old, was unconscious and completely unresponsive neurologically. His pupils were fixed and dilated. His EEG (electro-encephalogram), or brain activity tracing, was so flat I thought it had become disconnected. Jack had been connected to a respirator within moments of being admitted into the emergency room, and the respirator was taking every breath for him. His prognosis did not look good.

Dr. Shirley Meyer was Jack's primary doctor. I listened in disbelief to conversations she had with Claren, Susan, and Jennifer. Maybe she had some miracle cure none of the rest of us had ever heard of. Or she was giving them false hope for some reason. Within a few days, after repeating the EEG, I asked her if she was going to begin preparing the family. She said, "I'm not ready to do that yet, but you can go ahead and start the conversation." The prognosis was grim. Jack was brain dead. Just over a week after Jack was admitted, I began the conversation with Susan and Jennifer. Much to my relief, they were ready and knew their father was not going to recover. Within twenty-four hours, Claren, Susan, and Jennifer were ready to stop the life-support systems. They had some difficult conversations, but all agreed Jack would be furious to be spending any more time in the hospital. That was just never his style.

The doctors wanted to wait for what they said would be just a little longer on the long shot that brain activity could recur. This sounded weird to me, so I went to the back of the chart and, sure enough, he had two major insurance companies. Jack had become a real money maker for the unit. I had a feeling the doctors would drag this situation out as long as they could, so I had a very straight conversation with Susan and Jennifer. The next morning they insisted the doctors stop all life support. Dr. Meyers was abrupt with me, and in fact had me be the one to turn off the respirator, stopping Jack's respirations. He died peacefully, deeply unconscious, within three minutes. Jack and his family were lucky—he was kept alive on machinery for only two weeks and a half weeks.

After this interaction with Dr. Meyer, I spent some time thinking about Jack, his family, and all the circumstances. This family had rallied around Jack, and from my point of view, they had been loving and courageous. I don't know if Dr. Meyers' refusing to turn off the respirator and having me do it was a personal or professional decision. She refused to discuss it with me. Her actions were not a surprise to me. Was it her, personally, or was it something in her training that made her unable or unwilling to face or confront death and communicate honestly and openly with Jack's wife and children?

Joe was admitted into ICU directly from the emergency room late one night. In addition to taking the report from the ER nurse, I glanced through the history in the chart while the paramedics were still there. Joe, who was seventy-eight years old, had been diagnosed with pancreatic cancer two years prior to this admission. He had refused treatment for his cancer; he had no chemotherapy, no radiation, and no surgery. His family knew what he wanted and honored his decision. My question for the paramedics was how he had ended up in their hands, and then mine. They told me his neighbors had checked on him, found him unconscious, and called an ambulance. The paramedics were legally required to try to resuscitate him at that point, which they did. They then took him to the local hospital, and that hospital recommended they bring him into Seattle immediately, since they did not have an ICU. The resident assigned to him chose the most aggressive form of treatment available.

Within an hour Joe was hooked up to every machine modern medicine had invented. He was on a respirator, and we put in an arterial line, a Swan Ganz catheter, an EKG monitor, a urinary catheter, and two IV lines. In addition to the IV fluids, he was getting blood, albumin, and plasma. Joe had dissiculating intravascular coagulopathy (DIC), probably as a result of the spreading cancer. In other words, he was bleeding everywhere, internally as well as around every piece of equipment we put into him. I was applying pressure around the IV sites, the arterial line, and the Swan Ganz catheter. I knew it was a futile effort; the gauze compresses were being soaked in blood as fast as I could rotate them, and applying pressure around some of those sites was dangerous. We just kept trying to pour blood, albumin, plasma, and IV fluids into Joe faster than he was leaking them all out. At about three A.M. I asked the resident if we were going to do this all night. Clarice flipped out. She started yelling at me, telling me she was a doctor, trained to save lives, and if I had a problem with that I shouldn't be a nurse. I asked her if she had read Joe's chart (knowing she had), and she turned around and walked out of the room without answering.

At seven A.M. I turned Joe over to Patty, the nurse on days, wondering about the sanity of the medical profession. That day Joe's family made the trip to Seattle, brought a copy of the living will, and spoke to the doctors regarding Joe's wishes. He had never intended to be a patient in any hospital. Two days later we stopped the machinery. Joe, still unconscious, died within minutes. He had insurance coverage, as well as Medicare.

I could describe many patients like Gloria, Jack, Joe, and Floyd. They are everywhere, in your local hospitals and mine. Stories like theirs will continue as long as we let them.

The critical care units were originally set up for acute, short-term care. But because of our love affair with technology, the lucrative nature of critical care for doctors and hospitals (thousands of dollars per day for each patient) and our views on death and dying, many people become long-term patients in these units.

Lola, a sixty-eight-year-old woman who looked eighty-eight as a result of the disease process, had multiple admissions into ICU over a period of several years. She had chronic obstructive pulmonary disease (COPD), better known as emphysema. Once she was incubated and on a respirator, it sometimes took weeks to get her back to breathing on her own. She was a quiet, passive woman who had complete trust in her doctors. Her average length of stay in the unit was three to four weeks. The longest I know of was 131 days, almost four and a half months.

Dr. Parker, sixty-three years old and formerly a surgeon, had been diagnosed with lung cancer several months before he came into ICU as a patient. Dr. Parker had a long history of alcohol abuse and was a morphine addict, emaciated and psychotic much of the time. His lungs were literally decaying in his body. You could smell Dr. Parker when the elevator doors opened onto the second floor where ICU was located. He was on a morphine drip to manage his addiction and also an EKG monitor, arterial line, and a respirator. When he was awake, he was nasty to everyone, including his wife, and almost always tried ripping out every line we had in him. Sometimes he succeeded, and, under doctors' orders, we just sedated him more heavily and reinserted whatever he had pulled out. His favorite trick was to throw his urinal, full or not, at anyone who came through the door in his room. We watched him slowly deteriorate. He weighed less than seventy pounds. Finally the drugs, machines, and hardware could not sustain his life. He died, tied to his hospital bed. His doctors had kept him in ICU for over four months.

The current, presiding system will not change this phenomena; there is too much money in it for them. If it is ever going to change, it will be because you and I are no longer willing to tolerate having our lives and deaths dictated by doctors, hospitals, and insurance and drug companies.

By not thinking and talking about death, we keep the current system in place. We have become a death-denying culture. It is ironic that death is not called death in hospitals. It is called expiring, and expired bodies are taken to the hospital morgue in a gurney with a false bottom, so that it looks like an empty bed, through back corridors and down freight elevators. That way we, even in hospitals, don't have to see, or confront.

Also interesting is that when someone dies, that person must be pronounced expired by a doctor. As a registered nurse, I found that insulting. It was insulting because, after all of our training, it seemed the hospital policy makers couldn't trust us to tell when someone was dead or alive. Then I realized making the expiration pronouncement was simply another source of income for the doctors—one more item for which to bill the patients' insurance companies and families.

Insurance companies make such enormous profits, they are willing to pay so we don't have to confront the cost in dollars. Thus, life, or more accurately said, prolonging death, in the face of a dismal, terminal prognosis is business as usual in today's medical culture.

When one waits until a crisis, and either oneself, a family member, or loved one is already a patient in critical care, it is probably too late to hope for death with dignity. A crisis usually leaves us in our most vulnerable state—unable to make an objective choice. This is when the doctors take over. They use scare tactics on the patient and guilt tactics on family members. The doctors slide right in, almost naturally, to play God with our lives, and we let them.

Breakthroughs in medicine, by making something like open-heart surgery possible, often make it standard operating procedure. We now have patients in their seventies and eighties having open-heart surgery, routinely. While I have worked with fine open-heart surgeons who sometimes turn down performing this type of major surgery on the elderly, there is always another doctor who has no such qualms, who wants the money.

Volumes could be written about how and why these practices started and why they are so entrenched as a part of medicine. Those volumes of debates, political actions, and laws could even be used to put off changing anything for another two or three decades.

As long as we put up with it, the death-prolonging, high-tech system will continue. As long as we do nothing about it and wait for the AMA, doctors themselves, or the government, it will go on. Basic, fundamental, sweeping changes are needed. They will not come from within the medical system. Progress and changes in the medical bureaucracy have not kept up with the abuses, questions of ethics, or accountability.

One of the major accomplishments of this system is that we are lining the pockets of the medical profession. The medical industry is big business, a multibillion-dollar-a-year business, fast approaching one and a half trillion dollars a year. There are many constituencies involved in the big business of conventional medicine; all are committed to keeping conventional medicine exactly the way it is now, which means keeping us under the doctors' scalpels and prescription pads. They have become a bizarre influence in our culture. They will do nothing to support health-care reform; they are making huge profit margins with medicine as it is practiced today, and as it has been practiced over the last several decades. They do not care about us.

American medicine has been called, by some, "The best medicine money can buy." But it is a system that has run amok. It has taken a path called science and technology, and in that diversion has stopped serving people and begun serving itself. Our refusal to deal with death as a natural, normal end to life has skewed and distorted American medicine beyond recognition. The quality of life has been entirely displaced in the fight by doctors for quantity, or length, of life, defeating their enemy, death, and supporting themselves in the style they've become accustomed to, which demands a lot of money.

Though many people know this, I want to make it clear to everyone that insurance companies make huge profits with medicine practiced the way it is today. Without insurance companies and coverage set up the way it is now, many of us would decline treatments that run into thousands, and hundreds of thousands, of dollars and we would protest many of the exorbitant charges. Either that, or we would pay the bills, choose less expensive forms of treatment, begin exploring alternative forms of medicine and healing, or begin conversations about death and dying before we reach seventy years of age. Insurance companies and the medical industry are in bed together; they have the system set up so that they win financially. With the exorbitant costs of health care, we are coerced by fear to pay the high premiums on insurance policies or stay in jobs we hate for insurance coverage since one visit to the hospital could bankrupt many of us. Insurance companies are just one more part of a complicated, parasitic industry.

In our recent medical past we had procedures that included drilling holes into the human skull to relieve headaches and dispel evil spirits and using leeches to suck the blood out of patients suffering from various maladies. In their time, these methods were considered breakthroughs. What I am suggesting in comparison is that we have simply moved to a more technologically advanced in superstition. We can't begin to see the current medical absurdity that we are in because we have already accepted it as the way it is, and even as the "truth." We must begin to question and seek other options and possibilities to get outside of the superstitions we are now operating inside of. Doctors, and the whole medical industry, are completely dominated by an old paradigm that is not working and, in fact, is obsolete and bordering on the ridiculous. American medicine has become about combating disease, prolonging the death process, drugging and cutting people, and has almost nothing to do with health and well-being, prevention, the totality of the human being, or healing.

There are now reports out that claim ninety percent of health-care costs are incurred in the last year of a person's life. Hundreds of thousands of dollars can be spent to have needles shoved in your arms, legs, and heart, a big rubber hose shoved down your throat into your lungs, another smaller rubber hose shoved down your nose into your stomach so you can be fed, a plastic tube shoved up your urethra to make sure to can still produce urine, another rubber tube shoved into your rectum to empty the contents in a less messy way (because by now you are incontinent of urine and stool), while you are having all kinds of synthetic, expensive drugs pumped into your mind and body while doctors study the effects of all this and hope that it works. By this time you are usually in four-point restraints; your hands and feet are tied to the bed frame so that you cannot pull out any of these modern, high-technology procedures which are now considered breakthroughs. You also have several sticky discs stuck to your chest, connected with wires to a heart monitor. Add to this the noise of the respirator and the IV pumps that make sleep next to impossible. Does this experience sound like it's worth hundreds of thousands of dollars to you? Is this how we want to spend our last few days, weeks, or months here on earth? If not, why are we tolerating this kind of treatment? I'll tell you why. Modern medicine has been glamorized and sold to us, much like war was glamorized and sold to us over decades. It is glamorized and sold by companies and people who make a lot of money from medicine being practiced like this.

Most of us succumb to medicine the way it is dished out to us. My father did not. When he was seventy-four years old, Dad had a myocardial infarction, better known as a heart attack. He had been healthy and in good physical shape his whole life. He had never been a patient in a hospital, and that included his birth. His mother delivered him in their home into the hands of a midwife. My father stayed far away from doctors and hospitals and that is, in part, how he accounted for his good health.

After his heart attack, and what seemed like an interminable two-day stay in a hospital, my father vowed he would never again be a patient in a hospital. After what I had seen in the hospitals, I felt my dad was unusual. He didn't seem to have the same attachment many human beings have to staying in this life in their bodies and doing everything possible to stay there, no matter what. He knew he was more than his body. He was also sure that he did not want a knife cutting his body from his breastbone to his navel and huge forceps prying apart his ribs so his heart could then be roto-rootered.

I had never seen my dad take a drug of any kind, not a prescription drug or even an aspirin. He wanted no part of the hospital scene. He had also never seemed to have much respect for doctors and our medical system, so it was no surprise that he wasn't going to listen to them now and that he had no problem in telling them no and in saying no to their professional recommendations. He unequivocally said no to doctors and hospitals. In conversations with him I sensed a deep contentment and satisfaction in his having lived seventy-four years. Not to say he didn't have regrets, but he had no attachment to making it to eighty-five or ninety, at any cost.

Two years after his heart attack, he died of a second heart attack. I still miss him and sometimes wonder if he might be alive today if he had had the surgery, but I also realize that is my own selfishness. The truth is, I admire and respect him for the choice he made and the courage it took. He faced his life and his death with dignity. He trusted himself and let that trust guide his actions. He engaged in conversations with his family and friends that left him in a place called completion. He died in his own home, in his favorite chair, surrounded by what he loved. I find his actions and choices unusual and heroic. We do have choices, and heroes are nothing more than ordinary human beings, like you and me, taking extraordinary stands on shaping and authoring their own lives and deaths.

A possibility for employees in the medical industry, if they really want to make a difference, is to have a hospice in every single hospital—a planned space for people to die with dignity and in comfort, if they can't be in their own homes. In nursing school we studied death and dying. We also read Dr. Elisabeth Kubler-Ross's books on death and dying. We were trained to be with people as they completed their lives here. I was prepared and willing to do that. There was no space and no time within the hospital system for that kind of interaction. Even with terminally ill patients, in the end stages of cancer or congestive heart failure, our job as nurses was reduced to needles, IVs, giving drugs, and insurmountable amounts of charting and paperwork. At most there were moments to have conversations for completion, to listen to people, to let one know he or she had gotten his or her job done as a human being, to let people speak of their accomplishments and their regrets, to let them know they were loved and made a difference. My sitting with patients once I was off duty was by default, rather than an important, even crucial, part of my job. If I could have consistently provided that kind of time and care for patients, it would have been heaven going to work everyday.

Another possibility for conventional medicine is to begin to look at and treat underlying causes for presenting symptoms. This alone would be a breakthrough.

Courage and willingness to let go of what we know are necessary traits to make a difference. Change will, however, demand this from all of us and many people in health care, from the doctors to hospital administrators. It will take telling the truth when a patient doesn't have a chance to survive. It will mean not always scheduling surgeries, stopping powerful, expensive drugs and machines used to keep the heart and lungs going, and telling the truth to patients and their families. It may mean taking time to listen to patients, supporting them in seeking completion and saying good-bye. It will mean providing comfort. It will mean stopping high-tech medicine in many cases. It will upset the drug companies. It will upset the insurance companies. It will upset the hospital system, unless they start providing hospice care and the insurance companies cover it. It will upset just about everyone but the patient and the patients' families. It will look entirely different than it does now.

This transformation could be compared to our country giving up a war-based economy to become a peace-based economy. It represents huge changes and chaos. It means taking on and overcoming mind-numbing inertia, resistance, and the cynicism of those who say it can't be done because they don't want to see this change come about. Letting go of what we know for what is possible will bring up huge insecurities, especially for those who feel they have the most to lose in the transformation. It also calls upon every one of us, going into the twenty-first century, to take accountability for our own health and well-being, to take our power back and away from the medical industry. We will make the difference, the medical industry will not.

The career that had given my life meaning and huge possibilities was the same career that killed me off, like it has killed off thousands of other nurses and some doctors. Sooner or later we, as a group, are going to have to confront what is appropriate and what is not appropriate.

It may be that the only practical application for conventional medicine is in the area of trauma and possibly vaccines. And that is it.

Consider, for a moment, the possibility that surgery, drugs, and death-prolonging machinery may be barbaric; that they may be the most primitive, invasive, violent form of medicine and healing on earth.

Four

TRADITION:

THE GOOD-OLE-BOYS CLUB

The important thing is to not stop questioning.
                                          Albert Einstein

*He who strays from tradition becomes a sacrifice to the
extraordinary; he who remains in tradition is its slave.
Destruction follows in any case.*
                                          Friedrich W. Neitzsche

Though we take it for granted, American medicine, as we
know it, is a new phenomena. Wrenched from the hands of
women in the early 1900s, who up to that point were considered natural healers, men and medical schools took hold and
took over. Women were barred from medical school. The new
age of science as God had taken hold and still holds today.

It is now called a breakthrough that almost twenty-five
percent of medical students are women or minorities, people of
color. This percentage does not represent a breakthrough of any
kind no matter what the "experts" tell us; it is a predictable,
incremental change and that is all. This country is not made up of

mostly white men.

Doctors have been trained in academia by a system that is outdated, archaic, and smacks of blatant sexism, classism, and racism, and produces cookie-cutter doctors. The AMA violently opposed accepting women as doctors and fought social change demanding birth control methods being developed for women, and, in fact, the "mother" of birth control was not only a woman, but a nurse. The AMA more often than not opposes any kind of social change or reform being called for by the public. The AMA looks out for doctors' interests and pocket-books. They do not care about the public. And they represent the healing, care-giving profession.

While working in a large teaching hospital, every year we would get a new group of medical school students, interns, and residents from all over the country and from other countries as well. I don't remember ever seeing a black male or female medical student, intern, or resident in all the years I was there. (This is as recent as 1990!) There was one intern of Asian descent and one resident of Hispanic descent. There is a huge clinic attached to the hospital, with many doctors working there. Not one of them is black. There were, however, two women doctors. Toward the end of the eighties, there were a few women medical students and interns, but very few.

Medical schools train our doctors inside a paradigm that includes science, drugs and surgery, highly technological procedures, and little else. Medical schools are run by men, for men. The small percentage of women who are accepted either adjust to the good-ole-boy system and become a part of it, tolerate it, or leave. There is no changing it. Those who have gone before don't want the new medical students, interns, and residents to have it any easier than they did. Or they made it through, therefore they think they are elite and everyone else following them should have to go through the same things they did and "pay their dues." It worked (they think) for them, so why change it? Besides, change is almost always upsetting, and their egos and high incomes are what they are concerned with. Could it be that the medical schools of this country have gotten the training and practice of medicine down to a cold, calculated science reduced to numbers, statistics, technology, machines, profit margins, and little more than masking symptoms?

If the essence of science is being open-minded, how did scientific-based American medicine become so closed down? It is the rare doctor who refers his patients to alternative forms of health care and alternative health-care providers, like naturopathy, osteopathy, acupuncture, meditation, yoga, diet and nutrition classes, or a chiropractor. Many of these holistic approaches are not covered by insurance companies. Why are alternative forms of health care such a threat to doctors, the AMA, the FDA, and drug and insurance companies? Is it because they are not revenue producers for the conventional medical system?

One result of the scientific, technological breakthroughs in the field of medicine is the fragmentation into specialty areas. The list is long, and in part includes oncology, urology, gynecology, psychology, psychiatry, pediatrics, obstetrics, endocrinology, ophthalmology, pulmonary, thoracic, radiology, proctology, physical medicine and rehabilitation, pathology, orthopedic, nephrology, internal medicine, infectious diseases, infertility, gastroenterolgy, ENT (ear, nose, and throat), emergency, cardiovascular, dermatology, allergy, vascular, bariatrics, plastic surgery, geriatrics, immunology, anesthesiology, arthritis, environmental, and family practice, just to name a few. There are approximately 250 subspecialties inside our cut-and-drug system of medicine. Now, imagine doctors from each specialty sharing patients and communicating with one another regarding those patients and whose specialty and which part of the patient's body takes precedence. Egos and money get involved here, and the end results for patients are frustrating and sometimes dangerous.

One simple example of this danger is the number of prescription drugs people end up taking, with different doctors prescribing different drugs. I promise you the doctors don't always ask, or make sure they find out, what other drugs you are taking. This fragmentation in medicine further supports symptoms being treated, or, more accurately said, human beings being treated like pieces for each specialty, rather than holistically. The tremendous breakthroughs that have occurred within the specialty areas, that could benefit all of us, get funneled back through the old system of money and egos and the impact they could make is dissipated and sometimes lost.

I worked with medical students, interns, and residents for several years, so I do have some compassion for them, personally. As far as I can tell, from watching them and through conversations with them, they are slowly bludgeoned to death over time. The hours they are required to work each day, and the number of years they spend in training, being sleep-deprived to the point of being mentally disoriented and dangerous, slowly drains them of whatever humanitarian reasons they had for becoming doctors.

At four A.M. one morning I had a patient whose blood pressure had been gradually dropping. I knew I needed to talk to his doctor even though it was the middle of the night. I put the call in, explained the situation, and Dr. Rome gave me the orders for the patient. While I was writing them down, I realized they weren't correct, that he was mixing my patient up with another patient, and that he was talking in his sleep. I told him to get out of bed, stand up, and wake up. We got the orders straightened out and he thanked me the next morning. Another doctor happened to overhear our conversation and shared with us that he had fallen sound asleep, standing up, with a scalpel in his hand during surgery. Fortunately, he was asleep for just seconds and no damage was done. Another doctor shared with us that while he had never fallen asleep in surgery, he had fallen asleep at the wheel and run his car up onto the center divider. Darren, who is a cardiologist and friend of mine, after reading this shared in a very quiet, sad way he had been a resident when his children were born and because of his schedule during his years of training had spent an average of ten minutes a week with his two children for the first three and four years of their lives. This could elicit sympathy, but I am much more interested in why these seemingly normal people tolerate and put up with a ridiculous schedule for years. Then even more strange is that many of them carry over their training schedules into their private practices as if they have no say in the matter of their work schedules and their lives. They sound a little too close to victims and martyrs for me to want any of these people accountable for my health and well-being.

There is also a percentage of doctors who never had a vision for going into medicine beyond living like their parents did, having country club memberships and Mercedes in their driveways; or they have significant others and families who are pressuring them to increase the family standard of living, also called, "Keeping up with the Joneses."

By the time doctors finish their training, most of them are thousands of dollars in debt (seventy-five thousand dollars was low-end to average for the doctors I spoke with). Many of them, by this time, also have mortgages and families. Their lives and medical practice becomes a matter of making money fast to pay back the loans and financial aid, just to get caught up, as well as to meet current living expenses and get ahead as soon as possible. Whatever dreams or visions they may have had were worn down over time, reduced to economics. Doctors, after investing up to ten years in their training, are compelled to defend the system the way that it is. To not defend it would be risking their livelihood and questioning a huge investment in time and money that they have all just made. Then we wonder about the high rates of suicide, drug abuse, divorce, and alcoholism among our "healers." Doctors may be among the sickest group of people in our society.

Maybe the amount of power, prestige, and money we give doctors isn't enough to make up for whatever they experienced in the process of becoming doctors. I could come up with a lot of reasons, justifications, and excuses, but none of those would make a difference or change anything. I am long

past trying to figure out the reasons for it; I just know that
something has got to be done about it.

Within the medical system there is an unwritten code. The
majority of doctors are male. The majority of nurses are
female. When the positions of power went to the doctors, it
was rarely, if ever, questioned. Looking back on the years I
spent in nursing, I cannot believe I was nice enough, or naive
enough, to not slap several doctors with sexual harassment
charges. I can't believe I tolerated some of the behavior I did,
from having a doctor run his hand up the back of my dress
uniform to having another doctor grab my left breast as I
passed him in a hallway, to sexual double entendres as
common conversation from doctors directed at nurses over
patients' bedsides. Sometimes these remarks were about the
patient and were made as if that patient were not present and
not a human being. I can't believe that I didn't take the
problem to an attorney and court, or that I was so resigned
about the prevalence of sexual harassment within the system
I didn't think anything I could do would change anything.

The only justification I can think of now was this kind of
behavior was just so common. And it's not that I took this kind
of treatment. I slugged the doctor who grabbed my breast so
hard I left him gasping for breath. He never touched me again,
nor did he ever bring up the incident. But this kind of treatment
is still common, though now it may be more covert. (I have
heard from many nurses that it is no more covert in 1994 than
it was in 1990). Because of the atmosphere of the hospitals and
the roles, where doctors are still definitely in positions of
power, sexual harassment is very common in the field of
medicine. The high turnover rate in nursing is just one indicator; the last statistic I saw indicated that over seventy percent
of nurses leave their profession within five years. A friend of
mine, who is an attorney specializing in sexual harassment,
shared with me that the majority of her clients are nurses.

A much more subtle form of sexual harassment happens
under the auspices of doctors examining patients. Young,

attractive women get examined by more doctors than anyone else in the hospital. Word spreads through the ranks of interns and residents and they use their position of power to justify the exams. I have seen this recognized then written off as "boys will be boys." However, these interns and residents are not boys; they are supposed to be men and professionals.

Another indicator of sexism is the fact that over two-thirds of the one hundred million prescriptions for tranquilizers and sleeping pills in the U.S. are written for women. It is so much easier to prescribe drugs than deal with any underlying issues. Prescribing drugs gives doctors a feeling they have accomplished something. It also clears one patient out of his office and space so he can get on to the next patient. Dealing with the underlying issues of the symptoms that people come into doctors' offices with takes more time than writing out a prescription for a drug; it is a money-losing proposition for the conventional doctor to be remotely interested in underlying causes, hence our cut-and-drug culture. However, today's patients are no longer willing to be treated as part of an assembly line. They are better informed and have begun demanding alternatives, and this is the dilemma facing the conventional medical establishment.

Inside the hospital, it is standard operating procedure to order tranquilizers and "sleepers" for every patient. What that means is that you, as a patient, are artificially put to sleep in the hospital setting, and this has gone on for so many years and is so accepted we can't even see it as odd, to say the least.

One of the new wonder drugs is Prozac, an antidepressant. So if you're depressed, there is a new pill for that. The number of prescriptions for Prozac is now rivaling the number of prescriptions written for Valium and Librium in the 1970s and 1980s. The drug companies must love it; their yearly gross sales are approaching 3.5 billion dollars just for antidepressants! In the meantime, as a result of these pharmaceutical breakthroughs, and the partnerships between doctors and drug companies, millions of Americans are being drugged, and personalities are being chemically altered. And because of all the years of conditioning, culturally, we accept it as normal and natural to put synthetic drugs into our bodies without even pausing to consider short-term side effects or long-term side effects which every single drug has. Is it simply easier for doctors to deal with people who are drugged? Perhaps they don't question or disagree as much as people not on drugs.

In our own complacency and impatience for fast, easy answers and quick fixes, we have supported a profession that has gotten way out of hand—even fraudulent and dangerous. As we become more accountable for our own health and well-being, we will simply not accept this mindless drugging.

Today, in Seattle, seventy-five percent of gynecologists (women's reproductive and health-care specialists) are men, while less than one percent of urologists (men's reproductive and health care specialists) are women. Open your local telephone book and check out this statistic for yourself.

Pregnancy, labor, and delivery, once a normal and natural process, has been completely medicalized, hospitalized, institutionalized, and taken over by men. Pregnancy, something men will never experience, is completely run by a patriarchal system. It is ironic that, going into the twenty-first century, pregnant women are told how to take care of themselves by an anachronism. And in the process all kinds of drugs have been introduced, from piton (to induce labor and speed up contractions so the doctors can hasten the delivery) to pain killers, IVs, episiotomies and forcep deliveries (to hasten the process) and drugs to dry up normal breast feeding so they can keep makers of baby formula in business. Men are giving women "expert" advice on pregnancy, labor, and delivery, even though they will never experience it and can in no way relate.

The cost of having a baby, without complications, has reached several thousand dollars though the natural, normal process of labor and delivery hasn't changed at all. Childbirth is a guaranteed big moneymaker for doctors, drug companies, baby formula makers, and hospitals. We have let them do this. Maybe it is time for women to take this area back into their own hands and get male doctors out of obstetrics and gynecology.

Home births and births attended by midwives have been opposed by doctors, hospitals, drug and insurance companies, and the AMA only because it means a loss of money for American medicine. There is no other reason. All of their other reasons, excuses, stories, and protests are just that. The medical industry has to come up with reasons why doctors are the only truly qualified people on earth who can deliver babies. They can't be honest enough to say it is simply a loss of money for them if you have your baby at home or in the clinic of a midwife or nurse practitioner. In a very small percentage of deliveries, there may be complications. But we all know there are hospitals and emergency rooms within minutes away. To use the small percentage of possible complications as a justification to stay inside conventional medicine is one more manipulation and scare tactic used by the medical industry to get our money.

Cesarean sections account for almost one in every three births. This is a much more predictable, easier, faster way, for the doctors to deliver a baby. It also doubles the price for every baby delivered this way. One out of every three women delivering a baby has major abdominal surgery instead of delivering naturally. Why deliver naturally, when it can be done so much more expensively with surgery and so much more conveniently for the doctors? C-sections, also, let the doctor feel he is in control of the birth process, rather than the pregnant woman. Men controlling the birth process and women's bodies—what century are we going into?

If you choose to have your baby at home, in many states you will not be able to get a birth certificate for your newborn without going to court. No doctors' blessing, no legal baby…

There seems to be a violent resistance within the medical industry toward using anything natural and a total lack of regard for natural human processes.

Plastic surgery, the fastest growing specialty, is putting on an average of four hundred thousand dollars a year in every plastic surgeon's pocket. Between the advertising business, drug companies, and doctors, we are creating a generation of plastic women trying to look like Barbie dolls. For who? For what? Besides keeping the surgeons, drug companies, and prosthetic companies in business.

As an ICU nurse, I reviewed the surgery schedule every day to have an idea of the number of patients we would be admitting and the types of surgeries. I kept noticing large numbers of women scheduled for hysterectomies, and couldn't believe there were that many women with that many cancerous or diseased uteruses and ovaries in my city. I even had nurses in other hospitals in the city check on the average number of uteruses and ovaries being cut out of women every week in other hospitals. Nationwide, over twenty-two million American women have had a hysterectomy, and this surgical procedure is happening today at the quick pace of about seven hundred fifty thousand per year. These numbers are twice as high in America than in any other country in the world. Over a third of the women in this country over the age of forty have had a hysterectomy (castration is the accurate name for this procedure). Why? Because it is a hip-pocket surgery for doctors, translated: several thousand dollars into their wallets for a quick stint in the OR (operating room), much more lucrative than doctors recommending alternatives to cutting out women's uteruses and ovaries. How many men are walking around without their testicles or prostates? Given men's abhorrence to the very thought of castration, rarely are testicles and prostates cut out. Still, doctors, for whatever reasons, feel compelled to castrate women. Estimates have been published claiming that fifty percent to ninety-five percent of hysterectomies are medically unnecessary. If only the conservative estimate of fifty percent is true, we are dealing with a couple of generations of butchers calling themselves doctors.

Doctors and drug companies have been experimenting on women's bodies with birth control drugs for years. Doctors have performed forced sterilization on women, while denying other women abortions. Doctors have been cutting off women's breasts for years, as a treatment and cure for disease. They call this procedure a mastectomy; it is a much more antiseptic, professional-sounding name than cutting off women's breasts. What kind of training, or cultural conditioning, can medical students and doctors be getting to in any way justify the cutting out of anatomical parts that identify women as women? Why are we putting up with this? What is the cultural message? How much longer is this going to go on before we stop it?

While abortion is a hot political topic, whatever your own personal view on the subject, it is important for you to know that over a million abortions are performed every year in this country. While doctors prefer the higher revenue from full-length pregnancies, they do capitalize on abortion as opposed to preventative treatment. Doctors and the medical system are making approximately four hundred million dollars on this procedure each year. No wonder the FDA and AMA are opposed to the morning-after abortion pill. Insurance companies do not cover family planning or the cost of birth control pills. This fact speaks volumes regarding who is in control and how preventative treatment for people in this country does not benefit conventional medicine's ways of producing revenue.

It is simply amazing that women in this country have let organized medicine, which is run by men, tell us what to do, what we need, how we feel, how we're supposed to look, and convince us that we need them and must trust them. All of us, but especially women, must stop submitting to the conventional, patriarchal medical industry.

Doctors have made themselves indispensable to the American public. I sat down to watch a thirty-minute sitcom with my daughter last week, and within that thirty minutes, there were three commercials with doctors recommending that pill or this pill. What doctors? Who are they? Where are they? How much are they getting paid for every endorsement they make? Why are the media and advertising companies so eager to promote doctors as all-knowing and all-caring? Is it so lucrative for them that they just cannot resist?

Combine our medical system with the drug companies and advertising and the combination comes up deadly. Add the insurance companies, the medical equipment and supply companies, and you can consider your health and your life in danger. You are being sold some "medical" product on television approximately every ten minutes. Given the incredible number of hours we spend (as a culture) watching television, how could we not be influenced by all the mindless advertising we are continually bombarded with? Add to this radio commercials, billboards, and magazines, and you may begin to get a sense of how surrounded we are by propaganda.

I'm even beginning to question the Food and Drug Administration. Although I thought they were there to protect us, they are starting to sound more like they're in business to protect the major drug cartels, keep them in business, and keep the huge profit margins growing. Who are the people who make up the FDA? What is their training? How did they get their jobs there? What are they committed to? Who are they accountable to? Are they hired and, if so, for how long? Are they elected? Why are they such a mystery to the American public?

We are on the threshold of a new awareness about our bodies, our health, and what we want, expect, and can demand from the medical industry. However, we have grown up so indoctrinated by American medicine, many of us cannot yet recognize when we are being sold yet another procedure, product, treatment, surgery, or pill that may accomplish nothing more than producing revenue for the health industry. We are completely programmed to run to the doctor for every ache, every pain, every worry. If you are questioning this statement, go count the number of medications in your bathroom or kitchen cupboards. It is not unusual for individuals to be taking three prescription drugs, plus several more over-the-counter drugs at one time. If you put the elderly into this formula, the numbers go way up. We also have thousands of over-the-counter drugs readily available. I have walked into friends' and family members' bathrooms and been stunned by the number of drugs in their homes. This is only one example that demonstrates the extent of control and authority American medicine has over each of our lives.

How does all this show up in hospitals? Doctors expect complete trust and loyalty from everyone and to be questioned by no one. To call doctors authoritarian is an understatement. When doctors find themselves in situations they can't control, or when they feel they have lost control, some of them resort to throwing temper tantrums, unwilling or unable to communicate in any other way. They refuse to have their "rightful authority" even questioned.

I had been warned by other nurses to watch out for Dr. Bernden. He was a thoracic surgeon, and many of his patients were considered high risk, either because of the severity of their disease or because of their age. Most of the ICU nurses felt he was clinically a good doctor and I agreed. However, whenever one of his patients wasn't doing well, he predictably went into a fit of rage, screaming at the nurse taking care of his patients, accusing her of murdering his patient, throwing things in the patient's room, usually right in front of the patient's family and loud enough for everyone in the whole unit to hear. He was unable to confront what may have been his fault or no one's fault. I wondered how I would react to him, and it wasn't long before I found out. I reported for work one morning and was assigned only one patient. Dr. Bernden had done thoracic surgery on a seventy-nine-year-old man, who was not doing well. In spite of the latest in high-tech equipment, monitors, and drugs, we couldn't get his blood pressure up to a life-sustaining level, let alone maintain it. After doing a quick assessment of the patient, I called Dr. Bernden's office.

Within minutes, he arrived at the hospital, stormed into the patient's room, didn't talk to me, ask me anything, or even look at the chart. He began screaming. His face turned bright red as he screamed at me, "Can't you do anything right? Do I have to stay here myself so my patients stay alive? You are killing my patient. Are all you nurses idiots?" His voice had reached a high-pitched shrill. I felt sorry for the family, but kept quiet, choosing not to defend myself at that time.

However, I followed Dr. Bernden out of the room and said I wanted to talk to him. He refused to acknowledge I'd spoken to him until I said, "You had better turn around and listen to me." It must have been the tone of my voice, because he did turn around. I calmly told him if he ever yelled or spoke to me that way again I would call the police and have him arrested for verbal assault. I really didn't know if I could even do that, and I didn't care. There was a moment, by the look on his face, I knew he had heard me. He never threw another tantrum again when I was even in the same vicinity. Sometimes I wondered if he was only like that in the hospital, or if it carried over into other parts of his life. I found out from another nurse who had worked for him that he had a high turnover rate in employees in his office and that his wife had recently committed suicide. With that, I concluded he must have been a screaming jerk everywhere in his life, not just with ICU nurses.

One evening while working in the emergency room, we had a man, in the midst of a heart attack, come in by ambulance. We put him in a bed, hooked him up to the EKG monitor, and quickly stabilized his cardiac rhythm with medication. After his pain level diminished, I transferred Mr. Hampton to a gurney and took him to the coronary care unit. As soon as I returned to the ER, I went in to clean the bed so it would be ready for the next patient.

Dr. Turner, who had treated Mr. Hampton, was swabbing down the plastic cover of the mattress with alcohol. I had never seen him lift a finger to clean up anything and started to tease him about it. I stopped midsentence when I realized why he was using the alcohol. Mr. Hampton was a black man. Dr. Turner saw the shock on my face and started to somehow justify his actions as I backed out of the room; I just couldn't listen to anything he had to say.

I walked over to the nurse's station, sat down, and put my head down on the desk, feeling weary. I wondered if there were other racial incidents I had been unaware of, then I realized most of our patients were white. I still remember feeling embarassed by this revelation. I knew the hospital had a solid reputation; I didn't realize that also meant whites only.

Another incident involved a surgeon and one of the best nurses I had ever worked with. I heard someone yelling, left my patient's room, closed the door, and stood for a minute or so listening to Dr. Kramer scream at Mary for killing his patient (this attitude must be contagious among surgeons). Mary looked like she was about ready to cry and before I knew it I was walking toward Dr. Kramer. I calmly put my right hand around the base of his neck, pushed him against the wall, and quietly told him to shut up and stop yelling, or to get the hell out of ICU because he was scaring every patient in the unit. Dr. Kramer's face was a deep shade of red as he stormed out, screaming and yelling the whole way. Mary looked stunned. I gave her a quick hug and went back to work.

I knew I would get a call to report to the nursing supervisor's office and that I might lose my job. But I was sick of the abuse from the doctors, including their attitudes, whether they were screamers or not. Sometimes the snide remarks and the condescending, patronizing conversations were worse than the screaming and yelling. I had never been called honey or sweetie as much until I started working around doctors, and I knew I was neither a sweetie nor a honey.

When the call came, I turned my patient over to the nurse in charge and told her I might not be back. She assured me I would be back and thanked me for finally standing up to Dr. Kramer. I walked into the nursing supervisor's office and knew I was in trouble when I saw both Christine and Marilyn would be meeting with me. They told me to sit down, then they were both quiet, just looking at me. I finally blurted out that I didn't know what Kramer had told them, but that he deserved what he got. Christine and Marilyn looked at one another, then at me, and both burst out laughing. Christine was holding her sides from laughing so hard and had tears rolling down her face. I finally sat down, in relief. Marilyn said that although my language was completely inappropriate, and that it wasn't acceptable to physically throw surgeons around, they were both thrilled that a nurse had finally "nailed that jerk, Kramer," and that he would be barred from ICU for three months. That meant anytime he had a patient in ICU, he had to have another doctor take care of that patient until he was released from ICU. That represented a decrease in his income for three months. A minor victory. I went back downstairs to the unit and got to work.

One of the funniest things to me was doctors' reactions to being turned down for a date. I was attractive, smart, and single, and I did get asked out by doctors from time to time. I always said no—it was a rule of mine. Before returning to nursing school, I had known doctors outside the hospital setting and generally found them boring and uninformed about anything outside the realm of a diagnosis, prognosis, or a medical textbook. I had a neighbor, Jim, who was going through a divorce; he was on his own for the first time and had no idea how to handle getting his clothes dry-cleaned or how to get telephone service and a telephone. He was a thirty-six-year-old cardiologist. So, I always said no, and my answer was usually met by total disbelief. Most of them were stunned to be turned down, like I was turning down the biggest opportunity of my lifetime. But, giving them the benefit of the doubt, culturally, doctors have always been considered a "good catch."

Think about how many parents you know who would have loved to see their daughters marry a doctor. I didn't escape this cultural illusion, either. Even my mother would have been happy to have me marry a doctor. I wanted no part of it. I also recall doctors' wives introducing themselves as Mrs. Dr. John Smith or Mrs. Dr. Bill Johnson, as if this title meant something. One more symptom of cultural conditioning and the respect doctors and their families have expected, demanded, and gotten.

Although there must be people who become doctors for bigger reasons, many are seduced by, or succumb to, big bucks. Medicine becomes about making money, then more money. The tradition of medicine, and the way it is practiced today, is one of the biggest scams of our lifetime.

There are places to honor tradition—they are called museums. Much of our conventional medicine belongs in a museum, with honor or not. As a culture, we are staggering under the weight of old, worn-out traditions.

Philosophically, we could even say that what's happened in medicine over the last few decades is exactly what was needed to get us to this point. But where are we headed? I don't see any revolutionary steps being taken, except maybe technologically. What happened to basics like caring, prevention, support, and compassion? And true healing, rather than masking symptoms?

While writing this book, I got a telephone call from a good friend of mine, Dr. Mark Cohen, a medical consultant, committed to redesigning health care in America. He wanted to let me know he had recommended me as a potential business partner to a doctor affiliated with a major sports team in the Northwest. Because of my training and background, Mark had told Dr. Martin Johns to be sure to call me; he knew I was the one for the job. I looked forward to Martin's call. I imagined him developing a clinic in the central area of Seattle, where anyone could get medical care for a nominal fee. My job might be to organize and put the whole thing together and to teach classes and workshops. I was dreaming. When Martin called and described what he was up to, I could have cried. He said he had an elite, sophisticated medical practice, but what he wanted to do was close it down and begin a brand new venture. He no longer wanted to work with Seattle's rich people; he wanted to step up to work with Seattle's wealthy people, and what he wanted me to do is enroll Seattle's wealthiest families in having him as their personal physician, on a retainer basis.

He offered me a lot of money, and I agonized, for about ten seconds. I declined his offer, was gracious enough to thank him, while feeling like throwing up. When I looked at what was possible, and what he was interested in, I felt the medical profession was even more crass than anything I had ever imagined.

I also had to face my own humanity again. For a few seconds, I felt the pull toward a secure, rather glamorous, well-paid position. I was also flattered by the job offer.

Clever man, though. He was already coming up with ways to beat health care reform and keep his income above a million or two a year. Martin was even smart enough to call me back about a week later to tell me he admired me, and that my book was probably antithetical to what he was up to. Perhaps he thought, with the acknowledgment, he wouldn't find himself in this book. When were these guys going to get it? Medicine wasn't originally about money. Martin is one more perfect example of the good-ole-boys club.

The overwhelmingly huge business of medicine and health care, as we know it, is just one way to deal with our health and well-being. It is not the only way, though it is the way we have been taught and what is constantly advertised. While it may be the paradigm we have grown up in, it is not *the* truth.

Taking care of human beings, rather than masking symptoms with drugs and surgery, sounds like a radical idea at this point in time. Providing preventive and basic care, which seems like common sense, instead of high-tech rescue medicine, is what is needed—what's being called for, now, going into the twenty-first century.

Most of us are healthy most of the time, but this is not the information we are getting from doctors, the AMA, the FDA, the drug and insurance companies, the media, and all the paid-for advertising blitzes.

It is in the interest of the whole medical community to have us thinking there is something wrong with us that only they can fix. In fact it has gotten to the point where I've begun to wonder if this may be their main purpose: perpetrating the belief that there is something wrong with all of us that only conventional medicine can fix. This mind set fits perfectly into conventional medicine, as we know it.

A fact that is rarely written or talked about is the increasing number of people who become seriously ill and die in hospitals because of iatrogenic (hospital- and doctor-caused) diseases. Another joke around hospitals, with health care workers, who over time develop a rather perverse sense of humor, is that if you weren't real sick when you came into the hospital, you will be before you leave.

The lives and deaths of human beings cannot, and never will be able to, be explained in mathematical formulas, chemical reactions, and statistics and treated with only scientific, high-tech gimmicks and gadgetry and synthetic drugs. We are much greater than the sum of all our parts. We have already gone too far down the scientific, high-tech road. It is time to bring humanity and the humanities back into medicine and healing.

When doctors finish medical school and take the Hippocratic Oath, the first thing they promise, above all else, is to, "First, do no harm." One of the next promises they make is, if they don't know what to do, they will do nothing. Doing nothing has been recognized in medical circles for centuries as beneficial. However, American medicine cannot face doing nothing. It is addicted to productivity, which means doing something. The ever-present prescription pad and operating rooms with their scalpels, the high-tech machinery that needs to get used as often as possible to get paid for, and all of this covered by the insurance companies, are just too tempting. The percentage of doctors who uphold these two simple promises must be infinitesimal.

Five

WHERE IS THE ACCOUNTABILITY?

When you were born, you cried and the world rejoiced. Live your life in such a manner that when you die, the world cries and you rejoice.

Chief Seattle

Where is the accountability for doctors and health care facilities? Good question. I couldn't find it, even while working within the medical system. Besides wondering how doctors could sleep at night after horrendous mistakes that they made, I could never figure out why some of them were ever allowed back into the operating room, or why they were allowed to keep their medical licenses. There seems to be some unwritten, or unspoken, law that once a doctor has survived the ordeal of his training, he should never again have to answer to anyone for any of his actions, no matter his level of competence or incompetence. Completing medical school, and any additional training, does not guarantee a consummate, caring professional. Nor is it a statement of integrity or honor. It means they learned, or memorized, enough of the material to pass the tests. Are medical students required to take courses in humanities, in empowering people, in being peoples' partners in health care and in preventative care? Do they take philosophy classes? Do they study the process of death and dying? Do they study anything besides science and technological procedures, surgery, and drugs?

We all have our pictures, or ideas, of what hospitals are. Basically, and generally, I think most of us see them as warm places of healing and people getting well, or as wonderful places to complete our time here and die. In fact, they are neither. I cannot think of a colder, more hostile place I have ever been or worked in. The best I can say about them, having spent seven years working in several hospitals, is that they are cold, statistic-run laboratories, committed to making a big profit. We have been their source of revenue and their guinea pigs.

I would like to return to a patient and incident I spoke of earlier.

After an especially upsetting incident, where the surgeon, known to the nurses to be dangerous with a scalpel, had wreaked havoc once again, I physically stopped in his tracks the doctor "in charge" of ICU. Bill Lukas, the surgeon, had nicked the aorta of a patient up from California for a simple hiatal hernia repair, and she had died. The doctor in charge of ICU, Nick Jorgensen, was a good doctor and a good human being. He knew what was coming when I stopped him. I asked him if he had heard the latest on Dr. Lukas and he had. I looked at Nick, and before I started speaking, I knew I was going to be begging. I said, "She died. She's going home to California in a box. She's married. She has children. Something has got to be done, and Nick, you've got to do it." Nick looked at me, then looked down. When he couldn't maintain eye contact with me, I knew he would do nothing to stop this dangerous surgeon. He said, "Syd, my kids go to the same school as his kids—we're neighbors. My wife is a pharmacist in our neighborhood. Our families are together in social situations. What am I supposed to do?"

At the end of the day, I stopped by the nursing supervisor's office. Before I said a word, I knew they knew. I didn't mean to, but I broke out sobbing. "Christine," I said, "something has got to be done to protect the patients." She asked me if I would be willing to write up a report. I wrote it up, for all the good I thought it would do, somewhat surprised at my own cynicism.

Other patients were in danger, and no one was doing anything about it. Dr. Michael Brandon was a manic-depressive and had attempted suicide again; he had been in a psychiatric unit in a hospital over the weekend and had refused to turn his patients over to anyone else. How could someone like this man continue to practice medicine, and why were his peers all turning their heads and ignoring the situation? The nurses were huddled, in discussion, disgusted and worried about Dr. Brandon. None of us went into nursing to protect bad, sick, or weird doctors. Another report was written in protest of another dangerous doctor.

Hospitals do have peer-review committees. A group of doctors within the hospital reviews a case, if, finally, the concern about another doctor's incompetence becomes general knowledge around the hospital. What these doctors are faced with, simply, is pointing a finger at one of their own. Because all doctors have made mistakes, have ordered extra lab tests, or done procedures or surgeries not absolutely necessary, they are unwilling to single out another doctor, maybe because of fear of retribution. If one of their own could lose their hospital or surgical privileges, or even their license to practice medicine, maybe they could, too. So they are very conservative and quiet in their approach in disciplining another doctor, or even in questioning his competency. They simply close ranks and protect each other. Their own survival as doctors demands they handle it this way. It's as simple as the old game we all play from time to time—you don't call me on my stuff and I won't call you on yours. Anything to maintain status quo, to not rock the boat, to perpetuate mediocrity—the way it's always been.

Left on their own, unprotected from dangerous doctors, the American public did the only thing it could do. When they thought they could prove that some kind of mistake had been made, they sued for malpractice. When I hear doctors complaining about their malpractice insurance premiums, I want to scream. What do they expect? Do they think they can be irresponsible, even dangerous, forever? Only the most blatant cases end up in court. Most of the mistakes and negligence go unreported and are covered up by other doctors, anesthesiologists, and hospital administrators. By not reviewing the questionable cases in their own hospitals, in not taking disciplinary actions, in not making public the statistics of dangerous doctors, medical malpractice lawsuits came into being.

If a private citizen has the courage, and the money, to initiate a malpractice suit, chances are he or she will be defeated. The doctors and hospitals join forces with the insurance and drug companies and spend hundreds of thousands of dollars to defeat the private citizen. In the event that a doctor loses a malpractice suit or settles quietly out of court, the hospital, state licensing board, and, of course, the private citizen have no way of knowing. Furthermore, malpractice litigation doesn't put an incompetent doctor out of practice or even require that he improve his performance or get retrained, if he needs retraining. There is no follow-up by state licensing boards or anyone else. Your doctor may have lost one or several medical malpractice lawsuits. Have you asked him? If you did, would he tell you? Would he tell you the truth? Why aren't these facts made public? Why aren't American citizens protected?

Each and every year in this country at least one hundred fifty thousand people die as a result of medical malpractice. (I believe this number is a very conservative estimate.) This number translates to 411 people each and every day—seventeen people per hour who die at the hands of doctors. Yet we hear and read very little about it. Isn't it strange that the medical profession is somehow exempt from press and media coverage? The doctors are protected. We are not.

One thing you can do to protect yourself and your family is to ask a nurse to recommend a doctor. We all have our lists of who we might go to and who we wouldn't send our worst enemy to. Physicians' and dentists' telephone referrals are not a good idea. Doctors and dentists (or hospitals) pay to have those names on that list. They are paid advertisements; they do not measure competence, nor do they identify the incompetent.

We've all heard of the AMA (American Medical Association). They recommend this, they recommend that, but who are they? How do they become members? Do they merely pay an annual fee? Are they excellent doctors, or borderline acceptable? Are they reviewed or checked on in any way? Are they all MDs? As a nurse I didn't question the AMA. Now I'm very suspect of the whole political organization; do they do anything besides take care of their own and keep the old practices in place for yet another generation? Members of the AMA are all dues-paying doctors. The AMA is based in Chicago and runs like a trade guild or union. The AMA represents the wealthiest profession in this country. It is a doctors' lobby group. It is there to protect doctors and policies that benefit the doctors, not you. The AMA has an annual multimillion-dollar budget for lobbying to protect themselves and to promote policies that benefit doctors and medicine as it is practiced today.

There was a report on a senator who was going after bad doctors. At the next election, the AMA contributed thousands of dollars to his opponent, who won the election. The results of this election enabled bad doctors to keep practicing dangerous medicine. The AMA bought off a senator, yet they want our trust.

The Joint Commission on the Accreditation of Health Care Organizations (JCAH) accredits and licenses hospitals. Who are they? Who are they accountable to—the American public, or the AMA, or an arm of the government? How did they come to be a part of the JCAH? Who pays them? The only thing I knew about them, as a nurse, is that they notified hospitals months in advance of their visits so the hospitals would have time to clean up and get everything acceptable before the board showed up. At least a month before their arrival, everyone in a supervisory or administrative position was crazed. This strange process seems to make no difference and in fact keeps everything status quo.

Two of Washington State's largest health care insurance companies, Blue Cross and Blue Shield, spent over six hundred sixteen thousand dollars last year lobbying lawmakers and "informing," or advertising, to the public. They announced that they planned to spend more next year. They are no exception. These health insurance companies, who keep saying they are committed to cutting costs, pay their top executives over five hundred thousand dollars per year plus yearly bonuses.

Medical-dental insurance companies are another conservative political force committed to their own survival. If you think they have your interests in mind, think again. Their financial survival depends on keeping medicine exactly the way that it is today.

There seems to me to be a huge lack of conscience in the American medical system which very few people are questioning. Doctors and health care facilities, supported by insurance and drug companies and medical supply and equipment companies, are going the way they've been going for decades. They are on rails (as in a train on railroad tracks headed one way), unable or unwilling to do anything else. What seems like a huge moral dilemma to me is nothing to them. So again, it comes down to each one of us, as an individual challenging the system, to take our health and well-being back into our own hands, without expecting anything revolutionary or even transformational from an old paradigm which is slowly dying off and fighting for its life, fighting to keep things the way they are. It is you and I who are drugged and put under a surgeon's scalpel, paying huge amounts of money and sometimes paying with our lives; it's up to us to derail them.

When my son was born, I was a starry-eyed twenty-three-year-old. I chose my doctor on a friend's recommendation. Looking back, I could cry. Dr. Thomas Wagner, an obstetrician and gynecologist, had a very busy medical practice. I usually had to wait at least an hour to see him for a three-minute interaction. I was healthy and in great shape, and I really couldn't figure out why he needed to see me as often as he recommended. But, being young and trusting my doctor completely, I just went along with the program.

He knew I wanted a natural delivery and intended to breast feed my baby. Labor started at 10:30 AM on December 21st. When the contractions increased in strength and got closer together, I called my husband Dennis, then Dr. Wagner. He met us at the hospital one hour later. To make a very long story short, I delivered a beautiful, healthy baby boy. Looking back on the labor and delivery, it was a nightmare for me, but only medically.

When my contractions weren't producing an imminent birth, Dr. Wagner hooked me up to a piton drip. This drug increased the strength and frequency of my contractions and that is an understatement. Dr. Wagner almost demanded I have a local anesthetic because the baby seemed big. At that point I was in too vulnerable a position to even think of arguing with him. He also ended up doing an episiotomy, using forceps to hurry the process along.

Just after my son was born, Dr. Wagner recommended that I not breastfeed my baby since breast feeding would ruin the shape of my breasts, and that I let him give me a quick injection to stop the milk production, since breast feeding almost always produced infection of the breasts. He also assured me he could give me a case or two of formula for my son from the store of supplies he had in his office. It hurts to admit that I let a doctor talk me into that, and that I believed his lies. I wish I could go back and do the whole delivery differently. The best I can say about it was that I never went back to Dr. Wagner, and I told everyone I knew to stay away from him.

Several months later, when I ran into Dr. Wagner on a local tennis court, he asked me why I wasn't seeing him anymore. I told him and left him standing outside the tennis courts stuttering, with his face a bright red. He tried to justify the whole process to me; there was no justifying what he had done. Only in hindsight did I see I had not been accountable for my labor and delivery. The brainwashing had worked on me, too, and I had given in to his salesmanship and the old adage, "The doctor knows best. And if you can't trust your doctor, who can you trust?"

Dr. Wagner is still practicing medicine and when I mentioned to two friends of mine who are doctors that he had delivered my first child, they shouted in unison, "Oh, no, Sydne, not Thomas Wagner!" They agreed with me that he was and still is an insensitive, money-driven man who runs an assembly-line business. I still get angry looking back on that experience and cannot believe women still go to him.

After that experience, the one change I did make was to see only women doctors, no matter what. Unfortunately, that is not necessarily a guarantee of any kind, because the women doctors have been trained by men, inside the same old paradigm, and after years of training, I couldn't always tell them apart as far as attitudes and practices. Overreaction? Maybe, but I felt, with women doctors, treatment and statistics might be more in my favor. I also wanted to support women in business anyway. Fortunately, I've always been healthy, so I've been able to keep my contact with the medical system to a minimum.

I have included this experience, though it took place twenty-two years ago, because nothing much has changed, except the additional technology and machinery that are now available. I have heard so many women describe their experience of pregnancy and childbirth with the same frustration as I had that I am appalled and saddened. Twenty years later, the same circumstances (although maybe worse) exist. Fetal monitors are now used routinely. Screws are driven into the babies' skulls before they are even born. Violent medical intervention now begins before birth. Cesarean-sections are on the rise. We cannot wait for the system to change; we must change the system, in part by not tolerating bad advice or bad care.

Breast feeding a newborn is one of the most natural, normal things a mother can do for her baby. In addition to bonding with her baby, breast milk plays an important part in developing babies' immune systems and antibodies. Doctors know this, and they have known this for decades. They recommend bottle feeding because they have been bought off by the makers of baby formula. It is a big business in America. We even export baby formula to other countries, under the auspices of caring about newborns in other countries and assuming we have the right answer to this issue. This is just one more example of our perverse medical system's arrogance and greed. It also says something about doctors' opinions on what women can offer newborns; it becomes one more thing doctors take away from women in their own greed for control and money. If a woman has trouble breast feeding her newborn and needs to see her doctor, this represents a small charge that doctors don't feel is worth it; it is much easier and more lucrative for a doctor to give the woman a shot and not be bothered by any problems she might have breast feeding. This keeps the doctors' schedules more freed up for higher revenue-producing patients.

I had a minor medical crisis a few months ago while out sailing for a day. Even though I've been on boats all my life without a mishap of any kind, in July, while rigging up a jib sail, my left foot caught on a line, and I went down. I knew I had wrenched the anterior ligaments on my left knee, and the inside of my right knee was bruised and swollen. I managed to sail all day, but when I got home that night, I knew I was in trouble. When looking at my options, I realized medicine hadn't changed much. I could go to a doctor, and I knew I would be medicated, first with an anti-inflammatory, then a muscle relaxant, and probably a painkiller. I wasn't willing to go that route. I did not want my body full of synthetic drugs for days. I iced and elevated both my knees, and the next morning called an acupuncturist I had been hearing about. Though I hadn't slept well and I hurt, I was proud of myself for braving a brand new kind of treatment. I was amazed at the results. Ten days and two treatments after the injury, I was back to running three miles a day. When I think about the traditional method of treatment of American medicine, I shudder.

What I can say, with that whole experience behind me, is that I was scared. My training, just like yours, is to run to an emergency room or a doctor's office, and get fixed. The feeling of freedom in taking a risk and discovering what else is out there for health care has been exhilarating and satisfying for me.

It is up to each one of us to make the break from American medicine. We are on our own. American medicine is taking care of its own. As long as its constituencies are making plenty of money, they're not concerned about you. If they have a drop in profits, you will hear from them via their multimillion-dollar advertising campaigns.

It is almost too easy to blame the system; the system is made up of individual people. Even doctors blaming their own system is letting them off the hook for being accountable, responsible, adult professionals. They may have become victims of their system, but they let it happen. Whether they sold out, tolerated, or simply survived the system, they are responsible for the mess. I still hear doctors whining about their long hours. I've never seen a doctor with a gun to his head being forced to work twelve-hour days. They may still whine about it but we don't have to listen. Doctors are whining about their malpractice insurance premiums. Right now suing an incompetent doctor is the *only* recourse a patient has. And their medical malpractice insurance premiums are a small percentage of their annual income. This is just one more indication of how much doctors are run by money and are whining about their incomes rather than providing care.

When a system as large as medicine doesn't govern itself

and allows no outside checks and balances, we are all in danger. The lack of such a system would be almost comical if the results weren't so tragic, and the cost in dollars so astronomical. How do we as private citizens tell a good doctor from a bad one? What is in place to protect us?

For all the love and compassion nurses bring into the medical profession, they are also a tough, cynical group of people, and I'm including myself. Though most of us don't start out that way, it doesn't take long for the medical system to get to us. For all the reports I wrote up on doctors I saw who were incompetent or dangerous, I felt that the reports and concerns and complaints made little difference. I was also considered a troublemaker and a loud mouth. I got labeled for speaking up to protect patients who didn't even know they were in danger. Some of the doctors trusted and loved me. Others avoided or ignored me, pretending I wasn't in the same room with them. Nurses, patients, and their families trusted me completely. Somehow, they understood that I was there for them.

There were always a few of us who were vocal. Sometimes, I was surprised I wasn't fired on the spot. By then, I realized I didn't care whether or not I lost my job defending patients. I was a single parent, not independently wealthy, but I knew I was employable. Throwing caution to the wind had always been one of my strong suits.

Not so for many other nurses, many of whom were and are single parents, dependent on the health care systems and their jobs as nurses for their financial survival. There is also a percentage of nurses in every hospital in the country who are here on work visas from other countries. If they speak up, they get shipped back to whatever country they came from. Their hands are tied, their mouths closed. They do tremendous jobs as nurses, but we will probably never hear from them as far as changing the system.

Just to function as nurses, we have to repress a lot. If you stop to notice nurses' faces, you will see they wear their compromises, their toleration and their resignation about being able to make a difference in the medical system. They are a huge part of the system, and from my perspective, the best part. But nurses are not listened to in the system run by doctors. Nurses are highly trained professionals who dedicate themselves to taking care of patients and their families. Their bottom line is they are patient advocates. Most doctors do not relate to nurses in this way.

Because of cultural, sexual stereotypes, doctors almost naturally see the nurses as there for support for themselves, as their personal handmaidens. It wasn't so long ago that nurses had to stand when a doctor entered a room in the hospital; given the stereotypical roles that we have followed, I'm surprised the nurses weren't required to bow or curtsey, as well. So, in an attempt to take care of themselves, nurses quit nursing, or quit talking, and quit trying to change the system. Nurses have to trivialize horrendous mistakes and mistreatments they see made by doctors. Doctors as temper-tantrum throwers is just another bad joke among nurses. We watch doctors keep people alive, or follow "doctors' orders," and do things to patients we would never allow to happen to our own families or ourselves. If we don't, our jobs are in jeopardy. We mediate, placate, and begin justifying all that is happening, and often feel powerless to change anything. The huge cost of staying in nursing is in terms of selling out and compromising our morality and integrity.

As a nurse, I often had to act as an interpreter between the doctors and the patients and their families. The language used in medicine further alienates the doctors from their patients. It's not that diagnoses or conditions can't be explained in plain English; this is just one more way for the doctor to intimidate the patients. They use medical jargon to their advantage.

It seems that nurses are thwarted at every turn. We did not become nurses to push pills, do paperwork, and not have any time to spend with patients and their families. We became nurses because we love people and want to make a difference in the quality of life. Nurses work with people; doctors work with objects that they do things to. The integrity of nurses' visions and commitments is broken very quickly in the current cut-and-drug medical paradigm.

What's the answer to the accountability question? Simply that there is no accountability. The lack of integrity in this so-called honorable profession is so bad it can best be described as sleazy. Accountability will not come from within the medical system. There is too much pure survival at stake. Most health-care workers will hold on, no matter what, to the system they have always known, rather than confront the unknown. What they will attempt to appease us with is "new and improved" versions of the same old stuff they have been dishing out for years. Even accountability, and maybe especially accountability, is going to have to come from outside the system, and it is probably going to take every one of us to make any kind of a difference at all.

There are doctors accountable for themselves, the oath they took, and their patients. But these same doctors have stood by passively and let the incompetent, dangerous, and money-grabbing doctors trash their profession and rip people off.

Doctors are screaming to keep their independence, their fee-for-service charges (which produce exorbitant prices and encourage more tests, surgeries, treatments, and machines being used), and our trust. They are supported in their protests by the AMA, drug and insurance companies, the FDA, lobbyists, and medical laboratories—in other words, anyone who stands to lose money by changing the medical system in any way. These groups will fight Congress and whoever happens to be in the White House to protect themselves and their profit margins. Our health and well-being are not a part of their equation. They are looking out for themselves, and they do not care about you or me, except in terms of their own personal incomes. How much longer will we tolerate this? When will the madness stop?

Our health, and the power of making decisions about our health, our lives, and our deaths belongs to us, not the doctors or anyone else in the medical system. When you are in a doctor's office or hospital, you are not in custody. Those places are not prisons, although prisoners probably have more rights and freedom than patients do in any medical setting. We must take our power back and be accountable for our own health and well-being, because the medical profession is not. Yes, there are doctors who are exceptions, but they are either few and far between; more are concerned with their personal survival than making any kind of difference in their profession, our culture, our country, and future generations.

Though we are bombarded by media blitzes on how important it is to see your doctor, American medicine is not delivering on its promises. There have been no big breakthroughs in medicine since hand washing (which doctors resisted, sure that it made no difference), penicillin, and vaccines, and the penicillin, other antibiotics, and vaccines may not be the big breakthroughs we have been led to believe they were. Despite the billions of dollars being spent on research every year, there is no cure for cancer, multiple sclerosis, and many other diseases and illnesses; they are not even close to finding cures, let alone identifying causes. Medicine is not delivering on its promises, and it has not been delivering on its promises for decades. Yet, we are still buying the myths created by the medical industry.

The tide is just barely beginning to turn against conventional, American medicine in our country today; too many horrors of the system are beginning to be exposed. For example, we now know that forty-four percent of male doctors do not wash their hands after using the bathroom; thirteen percent of women doctors do not. This kind of arrogance is nothing short of astounding. The myth of a caring medical industry must be pierced; it is simply a lie. It is a package we have been sold over time. It is a package carefully, but forcefully, sold to us on every type of media available on the planet, twenty-four hours a day. The sale of American medicine is so pervasive, it is almost impossible to distinguish, and we cannot help but be affected by it.

We are the ones who can make a difference with this self-serving system. We cannot wait for the medical system itself—we would die waiting. We cannot take time to undo it. It must be undone now.

Six

THE COST IN DOLLARS AND CENTS

The test to which all methods of treatment are finally brought is whether or not they are lucrative to doctors.
George Bernard Shaw

Respond intelligently, even to unintelligent treatment.
Lao-Tsu

I am going to quote the current (1994) rates for a number of medical procedures and treatments. I hope you find them as shocking and unacceptable as I have.

I am including these costs because many of us are protected or insulated from the costs by insurance companies. We tend to think because insurance companies pick up a large percentage of the bill, somehow we're not paying for it. We also tend to not question the costs when we're only paying a percentage of the total bill. I don't think many people shop around for price in dealing with doctors, labs, hospitals, or prescription drugs. We've been conditioned, for years, to just pay up, whatever the amount. And yet, the difference of costs in the same procedure, with the same set of circumstances, can vary as much as several thousands of dollars from doctor to doctor and hospital to hospital.

If you have ever gone through the billings for a hospital stay, plus the doctors' bills which are separate, plus any bills from specialists called in, including radiology, you'll probably agree that, at best, it's confusing, and at worst, it's a nightmare, so you don't bother. Even I cannot believe this is intentional, and yet... I'm beginning to wonder if this is indeed an intentional smoke screen to make it confusing enough that we remain complacent about the charges. Even with my training and background in the medical system, it is nearly impossible for me to decipher charges or billings from doctors, hospitals, and insurance companies. I have friends who have been generous enough to let me look over their charges, billings, and statements and they are a nightmare to figure out. I almost stopped before I even got started a few times because of the amount of paper codes, generic as well as commercial names for drugs, medical terminology, and jargon involved. It was a mess.

Something I found that I did not expect to find was that people were paying their medical bills even though they had no idea what some of the charges were for. They could have been double-billed, or even triple-billed, for some of these things and never have known it. When I asked them if they handled other bills this way—say for example, car repairs, their credit card bills, or even restaurant bills—they all said no. Why are we so willing to pay medical bills we do not understand, when we don't really know if they are accurate, or even if they are ours? Are we afraid to not pay up? Is there some sort of fear or intimidation built into doctors, hospitals, and their billing practices? Maybe in the background, the thought is that if we don't pay up, whether or not we know what we're paying for, we won't receive care next time we need it. It may also be as simple as not wanting to look stupid, like we should be able to understand it. Or, because of the mostly impersonal nature of the medical system, the relationship between patient and doctor does not lend itself to questions being asked or any meaningful dialogue between hospitals, doctors' offices, and patients.

The results of a state audit of well over four thousand hospital bills was recently released. The audit found errors in 98.1 percent of the bills. The errors were all in favor of the hospital. The average amount of overbilling was one thousand, twelve hundred and fifty dollars. Ninety-seven percent of the bills contained charges for services that were never performed. Could this be intentional or is it merely a showing of gross imcompetence? If this were another type of business, criminal intent would be a consideration.

The following charges are random from different doctors and several hospitals and clinics. I have to add that these charges were not easy to obtain. No one (in hospitals or clinics) was eager to share this information with me; in fact, some of them sent me on hours of telephone calls, which led to dead ends. I contacted one organization that charged three hundred seventy-five dollars for releasing charges to the public. It was more frustrating than I ever imagined it would be. Apparently, they think what hospitals charge us is none of our business, until we get billed for something and they want their money immediately. Why do they protect their charges and fees like they are guarding gold in Fort Knox? Why don't they want us to know? What don't they want us to know?

> Doctor's office visit—$101.00; approximate time with doctor, 5-10 minutes.
>
> Specialist office visit—$137.00; approximate time with doctor, 5-10 minutes.
>
> Well patient checkup—$255.00; approximately 15 minutes with doctor plus lab work charges
>
> Emergency room visit (basic charge)—$234.00
>
> Emergency room doctors charge—$195.00
>
> Hospital bed, per day—$617.00
>
> Telemetry room—$812.00
>
> Bed in ICU, per day—$2,000.00
>
> Eggcrate mattress pad, foam rubber—$45.00

Chest x-ray—$101.00
Mammogram—$190.00
Cardiac catheter—$4,370.00
Swan Ganz catheter—$724.00
Saline solution—$27.00 (this is basically salt water)
TPN solution, per bag—$156.00
Barium enema—$382.00
Upper G.I. endoscopy—$983.00
Bronchoscopy—$800.00
Colonoscopy—$1,450.00
Band-Aids per box—$47.00
Abbott pump (for IVs)—$45.00 each
Lab drawing fee—$17.00
EKG—$87.00
 EKG interpretation—$26.00
Echocardiogram—$760.00
Cat scans, head—$849.00
Cat scans, abdomen—$985.00
V/Q scans—$855.00
MRIs each (abdomen, head, spine)—$1,617.00
X-ray for suspected fracture hand—$77.00
X-ray, sinuses—$183.00
EEG—$365.00
Respirator, per day—$354.00
Normal pregnancy, labor, and delivery—$4,000.00-
 $6,500.00
Normal pregnancy, labor, C-section delivery—
 $7,500.00-$11,000.00
Hysterectomy—$5,000.00
Appendectomy—$2,000.00
Arthroscopic knee surgery—$7,351.00 (60 minutes
 in OR, 4 ½-hour hospital stay)
Hernia surgery—$3,641.00 (20 minutes in OR, 2 ½-
 hours total hospital stay)
Cataract surgery—$4,100.00 (30 minutes in OR, 2-
 hour hospital stay)
Breast implants done in a doctors' office—$5,500.00

Vasectomy done in a doctors' office—$600.00
Nose surgery—$3,500.00
Facelift—$5,000.00-6,500.00+
Cardiac output setup—$84.00 (consists of a syringe
  and tube)
Routine labwork, on admission to ICU—$500.00+
Hospital charges for commonly used drugs:
 Streptokinase—$300.00 per dose
   TPA—$3,000.00 per dose
   Ticarcillin—$195.00 per dose
   Amikacin—$395.00 per dose
   Acyclovir—$295.00 per dose
   Digoxin immune fab—$7,435.00 per dose
   Albumin—$175.00 per dose
   IV immune globulin—$2,250.00

Some of these medications are given as many as six times
a day, over ten to fourteen days.

In July of this year a very good friend of mine was involved
in a fender bender. His Jeep was rear-ended. Dwight hit the
steering wheel and bruised his shoulder. He was taken by
ambulance to the nearest hospital emergency room, less than
three blocks away. On the ninety-second ride he was given no
drugs, no oxygen, no IV; in other words, he was not treated,
only transported. His bill for the ninety-second ride was
$650.00.

Last winter, in Seattle, we had an unusually strong wind
storm. A local man was hit by a falling tree, injured, and taken
to a nearby emergency room. The injuries he suffered left him
a paraplegic, paralyzed from the waist down. On an evening
news television show, the anchorman was asking for dona-
tions to help with his medical bills. He had been hospitalized
for less than a month and his medical bills already totaled over
five hundred thousand dollars, which is seventeen thousand
dollars a day, $708.00 an hour, twenty-four hours a day.

When I was born in 1948, my parents paid a bill of

$179.00, which included doctors' charges, hospital fees, labor and delivery room, a semiprivate room for my mother, lab charges, the nursery, and medications over a four-day hospital stay. My friend, Michelle, had a baby last fall. It was a natural, vaginal delivery, which included a two-day hospital stay, and the total bill was $5,780.00. If she had had a Cesarean-section, her bill could have been closer to $10,000.00! Her charge of $5,780.00 is $5,601.00 more than a birth cost two generations earlier. This is over a thirty-one hundred percent increase— for what? The process is exactly the same as it always has been. What are we paying for?

A patient facing a bone marrow transplant can expect to pay several hundred thousand dollars, and the hospitals want cash, because some insurance companies don't cover this procedure. As a culture, we had better hope that only the wealthy will ever need bone marrow transplants because they are the only ones even able to consider this treatment.

I took my daughter in to get contact lenses last week. The total bill was $310.00. The ophthalmologist spent less than five minutes with her. The rest of the time a young woman, who probably makes seven dollars an hour, worked with her for less than an hour, and this amount of time included both appointments. The tinted lenses that we ordered didn't get ordered; no one knew why, no one called to let us know so that we could reschedule the second appointment, no one apologized for the inconvenience to us (I had taken two afternoons off work), and, to top it all off, they wanted their money in full immediately. Absolutely unbelievable from a profession that was once about service.

I am including prices from the dental field—they are shocking, as well. I broke an old, large filling, and I needed a root canal and a crown. The root canal was $400.00 ($700.00 if I wanted to go to a specialist). I needed a post and buildup, another $120.00, and the crown was $600.00. One thousand, one hundred and twenty dollars for one tooth! The x-rays were extra... Now, I could have had that tooth extracted. Within months, my bite, or occlusion, would have been out of kilter.

Then, I would have needed a bridge that cost two thousand dollars. Some choice.

Several days ago, on the evening national newscast, a report was issued that stated millions of Americans were suffering from various dental diseases. They simply could not afford to see their dentists. Maybe it is time for dentists to wake up to the fact that they are pricing themselves out of business.

Oral surgery, also included in health care coverage, is every bit as ludicrous. A friend of mine was referred to an oral surgeon by her dentist. She needed to have a tiny bone spur removed to have a crown successfully set. The seven-minute procedure cost her $450.00 plus a $165.00 charge for an IV drug, administered for less than five. Most people don't know that many doctors own, or own a percentage of, medical laboratories and medical supply and equipment companies. This fact, in part, could account for the long list of lab tests that are routinely ordered everyday, day after day—one more way of producing revenue that doctors take advantage of.

Another not-well-known fact is that doctors work out "deals" with hospitals. Our doctors don't necessarily admit us to the best hospital; they admit us to the hospital where they get the best deal in dollars, perks, and benefits, or to a hospital where they have an agreement to admit a certain number of patients per month. Yes, as patients we are often part of a quota system between doctors and hospitals. Most of us do not know our bodies are being brokered at the same time we're being treated. Again, and always, money is the determining factor in health care.

Coronary artery bypass grafts, better known as open-heart surgeries, may relieve symptoms for a while, but may do nothing to prolong life. There have been studies out for years that open-heart surgery may make absolutely no difference for the patient, and if the patient lives for very long, he or she will need to repeat the surgery. Diet and exercise are thought, by some studies, to be more effective than surgery. However, managing chest pain with diet and exercise provides no money for doctors and hospitals, so doctors are not going to be eager to promote alleviating symptoms with something as simple as exercise and food. They would be losing thousands of dollars every time they treated a patient that way, instead of in the hospital, under a scalpel.

Doctors are performing more angioplasties (a less invasive form of roto-rootering the heart vessels). This procedure is nine thousand dollars. Latest reports claim sixty to seventy percent of the four hundred thousand angioplasties done every year in this country are medically unnecessary—another hip-pocket procedure.

Recently, in a local newspaper, there was a story written about a doctor working at a medical clinic in Illinois. He was fired by the clinic because the owner of the clinic felt he wasn't charging enough for his services, ordering enough lab tests, or doing enough surgeries to produce the kind of money they expected him to. He was even sensitive enough to be aware of people's ability to pay and adjusted his charges accordingly. He didn't do every lab test or blood test available on the planet if he didn't feel they were necessary. Even though his patients loved and trusted him and by all accounts he is a superb doctor, he was made to pay for not conforming to what medicine has become about today, which is making big money. He left the clinic, opened up his own office, had patients who loved him follow him to his new location, and is now being sued by the clinic that fired him. This is just one instance of a competent, caring doctor not following a set of prescribed rules all set around making a lot of money, who lost his position in a medical clinic set up to rip off the public. The amazing, or maybe not-so-amazing, aftermath is that the clinic he was fired from is still after him, attempting to make money off of him.

I don't care how the medical system tries to justify these numbers. There is no justifying them. The American medical system has been financially and emotionally raping the citizens of this country long enough.

The definition of a patient is "someone *under* medical

treatment." The definition of under is "in a lower position or place than." Perhaps it is time to come up with a new name, one that at least implies equality and partnership.

The definition of doctor is "a person who has earned the highest academic degree; a person trained in the healing arts." Healing and arts no longer fit into American medicine and doctors as they are today.

Although we call medical insurance "health" insurance, it has almost nothing to do with health. Why not change the name so it reflects what it is about? We could call it disease insurance, or trauma insurance, disaster insurance, "fear or what if" insurance, but not health insurance, since there is nothing healthy about it.

Another thing to take into account is how much the insurance companies are making today. There have got to be huge margins of profit for them to be so firmly entrenched in the business. If there weren't, they wouldn't be fighting so hard to keep things the way they are. The insurance industry wouldn't have lobbyists in Washington D.C. spending millions of dollars to keep Congress gridlocked. They wouldn't be spending millions of dollars for commercials on television to put down every attempt at reform of any kind. I have spoken to doctors who have come to feel that their medical practices are completely run by the insurance companies. Why are they tolerating this? Why are we tolerating this? A single-payer system is their worst nightmare—it would render them obsolete. Another fascinating aspect to the whole insurance industry fiasco is that we now need experts to decipher the policies and find all the loopholes. There are several long, heavy books out now in an attempt to support the consumers and explain all the different kinds of policies offered by over fifteen hundred different insurance companies.

The drug companies are a multibillion-dollar-a-year business. The legal drug business is the most profitable business in this country. Representatives from the drug companies have tried to justify this by saying most of the money goes for research and development. In reality most of the money goes for sales, promotion, advertising, and courting doctors. There are over fifty thousand salespeople selling drugs from doctor to doctor and hospital to hospital. Markups on drugs run anywhere from two to three times the cost to thousands of times the cost. In the years I worked as a nurse, I was offered jobs several times by drug companies. Though I was amazed at the salaries and benefits, which were much better than what I was making as a nurse, I couldn't reconcile selling drugs for a living. It was also stunning to me the number of boxes and bottles of free samples of drugs the drug reps left with the doctors on each visit—all as an inducement for the doctor to prescribe their particular drugs from their company. Recently a major drug company contributed thirty million dollars to support people in Rwanda. While I applaud their actions, it would have made much more sense if they had donated the money on behalf of the American people instead of it being another advertising plug for their particular company. The drug companies are another parasitic aspect of the medical industry.

There are so many factions involved in, and contributing to, American medicine, it is difficult to keep track of all of them. They have a huge amount of time and money, as well as ego, invested in keeping medicine the way that it is now. They have no reason to want to change it, no reason to have our interests at heart. As long as they keep making money, they will not stop. As long as we keep blindly trusting American medicine and American doctors, it will go on. It is big business, as usual, in America. The one distinguishing factor is that this business involves our health and bodies. Our lives and our deaths are at stake here. If we don't take accountability, there will be no accountability. American medicine is a huge, lumbering, conservative, greedy bureaucracy. As long as we acquiesce to it, it will keep cutting and drugging us and billing our insurance companies. We must stop paying these ridiculous, obscene prices.

Seven

THE POLITICS BEHIND THE
POLICIES

Every man takes the limits of his own field of vision for the limits of the world.

Arthur Schopenhauer

Nothing is ever accomplished by a reasonable man.
George Bernard Shaw

The politics of medicine began with the birth of the AMA in 1847. A group of doctors got together, formed the association, and the politics began. The AMA began the "doctor knows best" slogan that we know so well today. They also began attacking, with the intent to eliminate, all alternative (not allopathic) forms of healing and health care. By the early 1900s, armed with money and aligning themselves with the politics of the day, while exploiting science and technology, they became the monopoly that has been sold to us for decades.

The politics of medicine have become a reflection of the

politics of the country. Most of the positions of power are held by old, white, conservative, wealthy, heterosexual men. They still think they represent us, but they don't. When I turn on the news and hear some of the conservative old men defending our medical system as the best in the world, I feel I am inescapably surrounded by evil or thoughtless people pretending to represent us. They are so out of touch with reality and American citizens, it is time for them to retire or take their blinders off and begin listening to what the American citizens want. I sometimes wonder what our founding fathers' reactions would be to the politics of today's medical industry. Did they intend for the one with the most money to win every election? Did they intend for the ones with the most money to be governing this country and its social institutions?

Where is the division of power in medicine? Where are the checks and balances? Who monitors doctors and the AMA? What is in place to protect us?

While the majority of Americans are for universal health care coverage, our voices are not being heard over the cacophany coming from the congressmen who have been bought off by the big businesses and the lobbyists. And this is called democracy! The health care industry spends millions of dollars on lobbyists, the press, and other media to convince us they are on our side and have our best interests at heart or at least on their agenda. They don't. What they are engaged in is witch hunts and smear campaigns.

A part of their media campaign has been to destroy any perception we may have, as a culture, that the single-payer system works. They have spent millions of our dollars to convince us that Canada's single-payer system and universal health care coverage aren't working. The only ones this system wouldn't work for are doctors and drug and insurance companies. They wouldn't make the kind of money they have grown accustomed to making, and they wouldn't have the public adoration which they think they have now.

As a culture, we have broken out of the old cut-and-drug paradigm. The politics of medicine have not; they seem to lag a decade or so behind the conversation of the public. The distrust doctors and the medical industry have earned is apparent whether they recognize it or not.

Universal coverage with a single-payer system could eliminate the need for the parasitic insurance industry. There is over one hundred billion dollars in fraud in this industry alone. Nothing more really needs to be said. But remember, this whole system is set up so that the more that is done to you, the more money the insurance companies make. And it just gets worse. If the insurance companies decide you are a high-risk person, that you will cost them too much money, that you have a chronic condition that calls for continued care and medication, they can drop you without warning. If you are dropped by one insurance company, it is highly unlikely that you will be picked up by another insurance company. The insurance companies remind me of vultlures surrounding their prey, only the insurance companies are a bit more discretionary than vultures. Today we need an attorney to decipher insurance policies—what they cover and what they don't, as well as major loopholes in the coverage. The elderly who are covered by Medicare are being sold supplemental policy after supplemental policy so they at least have the illusion of being "covered" and can sleep at night in peace. This business of health insurance may be more in control of medical practices than the AMA and doctors are.

The story on the drug companies just gets worse. We pop more pills per capita than any nation on earth. Because of the millions of dollars the drug companies spend on advertising, media blitzes, and public relations, culturally, we see this pill popping as somewhat normal. The drug business makes more money than any other legal business on the face of the earth. They have a great deal invested in keeping medicine as it is. The more I have read and discovered about the AMA and the insurance and drug businesses, the more the word "pimp" comes to mind. We need to begin protecting ourselves against these big, political businesses. The AMA could be appropriately renamed the AMMA (American Medical Mafiosa Association).

The endless screeching by the congressmen, the AMA, and the insurance and drug companies is simply the backlash before the end of medicine as we have known it—the end of obscene profits and the end of American people being used as commodities for the perverse practices of conventional medicine. Conventional medicine is not the best medicine money can buy; it is the most expensive. There is talk of quality assurance going out the window with universal health care coverage. There is no quality assurance now. None.

There are so many alternatives to American medicine available and yet we rarely hear about them. The media and advertising don't cover them. Last week, in a weekly news magazine, there was a cartoon depicting alternative health care providers as witch doctors. Who is paying for this? What message are they trying to send? Why is conventional medicine so afraid of alternatives?

There is a tight circle between the big business of medicine, the FDA, the AMA, lobbyists, doctors, hospitals, and drug and insurance companies. They don't want anyone else (like private American citizens) included in this loop. They spend millions of dollars to buy off elected officials and keep Congress gridlocked so that reform of any kind is not possible and is kept on a kind of eternal hold. They have been successful for thirty years. And we call this democracy? It is closer to a travesty.

It is time to stop the political games being played. It is time for elected officials to do what they were elected to do—serve the public. Very simple, right? Wrong. Health care reform is being called the most daunting, confusing political issue Americans have ever faced. This is being played out in Congress and the media as one more ploy, tactic, or strategy to protect big business. America's health-care system is an abomination. It is time to stop the insanity and the terrorist tactics. And it is up to us.

We could let the medical industry keep fighting its greedy political battles. Maybe it will kill itself off in its long-winded rhetoric. Medicine has become about money, for money, and it is defended by money. It has nothing to do with health or healing.

It is always a mistake to underestimate human beings. This country was founded on a revolution. Perhaps it is time for another one.

Eight

BREAKING OUT OF A CULTLIKE

SYSTEM

The doctor of the future will give no medicine, but will interest his patients in the human frame, in diet, and in the cause and prevention of disease.

Thomas Edison, early 1900s

The important thing is this: to be able at any moment to sacrifice what we are for what we could become.

Charles Dubois

The medical industry has done an effective job of brainwashing us. This industry has spent decades and billions upon billions of dollars to do so. "Doctors recommend..." has become an established badge to flash in the marketing of visits to doctors, hospitals, and clinics and the number of tests, procedures, surgeries, and synthetic drugs prescribed as the way of life in America.

They have sold us a bill of goods and promises they have not, and cannot, deliver on. Take this pill, it will take away the pain; take that pill, it will help you sleep; take this pill, it will wake you up; take that pill, it will regulate you; use this particular brand of soap or deodorant, it will change you life. "Doctors recommend…" Stop and think for a moment how many times a day we hear or read that. How many times last fall and winter did we hear, via media campaigns, that "It's the flu season!" or, "The cold season is upon us!" on the radio and television? Doctors are now declaring speceal medical seasons, which imply the immediate need for doctors, drugs, pills, injections, or even hospitals, if you happen to be older. Quick fixes and drugs as a way of life are what we are being sold through billions of dollars of advertising and propaganda. They are attempting to convince us that there is something wrong with us or scare us into believing we need them, just to be prudent and safe. God forbid we should have to face a flu or cold season without them.

Advertising and statistics are used to herd people to doctors at least once or twice a year for checkups because of all the lurking, dangerous possibilities and symptoms. This sounds a little like weird science fiction to me. Scare tactics and terrorist tactics are being used to produce more business and revenue for the greedy medical industry. Many ancillary industries surround and feed off of medicine, all the while putting our health and well-being at risk.

Hospitals are now advertising their services and their own particular brands of humanitarian care and treatment. Medical clinics are advertising, doctors are advertising, as are plastic surgery clinics, emergency medical treatment centers, back clinics, allergy clinics; the list goes on and on. They have launched huge advertising campaigns to convince us that we need them. They are vying for our money. They are in competition with each other over who will get the greatest number of patients, the fastest. They must keep up the volume, the number of people they see, to maintain their incomes, to pay for their billions of dollars of high-tech equipment, their huge medical-industrial complexes, parking garages, art and real-estate investments. They need us to be ill, or to at least have some symptoms for which they can treat us. We have been manipulated, used, and coerced by out revered medical system.

The whole medical industry has shaped and developed a culture that is focused on illness, disease, and prolonging life or avoiding death no matter what the cost. Through the indoctrination process, mostly advertising, and some education, we have become a culture that believes there is something wrong with our bodies or our faces that only American medicine can take care of, whether that includes drugs or surgeries. Doctors are going to do what they are trained to do—cut or drug. They have the support of every medical school, hospital, clinic, drug company, laboratory, insurance company, medical equipment and supply company, the FDA, the AMA, and many politicians, special interest groups, and lobbyists.

If you have any doubts about the effects of advertising, I am going to dispel them now. As a student nurse, I worked in two different doctors' offices. Every month several women's magazines had articles on women's "health." In reality, they each had an article that focused on some major disease or some lurking, devastating health hazard with all the accompanying symptoms. Depending on the articles of the month, we came to naturally expect a barrage of calls and subsequent appointments from women who had read the articles and were headed to doctors in droves. We could even predict, based on the magazine articles, what their presenting symptoms and complaints would be. I remember, vividly, the doctors laughing, loud and long, at the women and their gullibility and susceptibility to these published, so-called respectable articles—not to their faces, of course, but at the end of the day or end of the week, as they counted the money they had made. The only comparable experience for men is chest pain and the "ever-present" threat of heart attacks. Working in the emergency room as a nurse, this publicized, advertised threat for men brought them into ERs terrified. The overwhelming majority of these men had heartburn and indigestion, mostly from overeating. But the power of the press and terrorist tactics from American medicine were painfully apparent. They keep the medical industry's cash registers ringing.

Drug companies' mission is to sell drugs. There are more and more commercials everywhere—TV, radio, billboards, magazines. The drug companies are spending millions of dollars a year to shape your awareness and buy your business. The drug companies hold the honor of being in the most profitable business in America. Prescription-drug prices rose three times higher than inflation in the last decade. Through their "caring" for the American public, pharmacies are being built into our grocery stores. Drugs have become as important as food in America. Get your food and drugs all in one place. If you think they are doing that for your convenience, think again. It is a cold and calculated move on the drug companies' part. They are in business to make money. They do *not* care about us. They want our money. And they want us on their legal, lethal drugs.

In addition to the pharmacies inside grocery stores, the grocery stores dedicate whole aisles of their stores for all the over-the-counter drugs sold in America. There is hardly a food commercial on television that doesn't also include a drug to combat the effects of food. For every hour of television we watch, we are subjected to nearly twenty minutes of commercials, up to thirty-two different items pushed at us in a higher volume than regular programming. Almost half of the products advertised are drugs.

Then we wonder about substance abuse among our children. Could it be we are setting the example, though our drugs are considered legal? No one has been able to stop this mindless, greedy drugging of American people. The doctors and drug companies are accountable to no one.

The markup on drugs is anywhere from three times the cost to one thousand times the cost. In their high-minded justification of the cost of drugs, the choice is very simple—

your money or your life. They are truly the drug lords. They may be more dangerous than any illegal drug cartel, simply because what they are doing is considered legal and supported by the medical industry and some people we have elected to govern us.

Other huge multibillion-dollar industries are the medical equipment and supply companies. In an article recently published in a local newspaper, it was noted that the highest paid woman in America in 1992 was a woman who headed a surgical corporation. She was paid over twenty-three million dollars for one year of work in the medical industry. I don't know about you, but it makes me wonder. If medicine wasn't touted as such an honorable profession, maybe this wouldn't matter as much. If it weren't our health and bodies, our births, our lives and deaths, put at risk, maybe it would just be simply one more grossly mismanaged business.

All of these industries and companies are working together to sell us on how badly we need them. This sounds like a conspiracy or a cult. The dictionary defines cult as "a system or community of religious worship and ritual; followers of such a religion, or sect; obsessive devotion or veneration for a person, principle, or ideal; an exclusive group of persons sharing an esoteric interest." Conspiracy is defined as "an agreement to perform together an illegal, treacherous, or evil act." These definitions are perfect fits for our American medical system. If I wanted to take a different tack on this, I could say all of this was completely unintentional, that the medical industry simply evolved, or rather, devolved, to what it is today. That would imply that there is no one accountable for anything that goes on in medicine today. Though frightening, that in itself may be closer to the truth. What is the underlying philosophy in medicine? I certainly could never find it. It looked like one big money-making machine to me, with everyone racing around trying to get the greatest number of patients who needed the greatest number of surgeries or any other billable procedures and treatments.

A developing trend in medicine today is the Health Maintenance Organization (HMO). HMOs are being touted as a new, better way to practice medicine. I assert they are "new and improved" versions of the same old stuff, relabeled. They operate inside the cut-and-drug paradigm.

In an attempt to at least look like they are cutting costs and saving us money, the medical industry has begun another trend—cutting the number of nurses. This is dangerous and ludicrous. Dangerous because nurses are the caregivers for patients. Ludicrous because nurses earn around thirty thousand dollars per year while the average income for doctors is over one hundred fifty thousand dollars per year. Common sense, alone, dictates decreasing the number of doctors, especially the specialists, and increasing the number of nurses.

Medical training is designed to induce a state of helplessness and dependency in patients. This sets up the doctor as a dominating authority and expert, trained to serve and preserve his profession and medical institutions. It also sets up anyone who is a patient as a commodity.

A friend of mine, Dr. Jim Myers, is at this time facing charges from other doctors in a small town in the Northwest and will be in front of the medical disciplinary board this month. His "crime" is that two years ago he began to suggest alternative forms of care for his many patients. He had a thriving private practice and hundreds of patients who loved him. The alternative forms of care he suggested were as simple as diet, vitamins, exercise, and massage therapy, instead of drugs and surgery. First he found himself confronted by the hospital board because he was not admitting enough patients to the hospital. He also found himself confronted by other doctors in the community, because they were losing patients to him. People in this community flocked to Jim and the other doctors became jealous. His success in treating patients also meant a loss of revenue to doctors who were losing patients to Jim. Rather than find out what he was up to and why people were choosing to go to him, they simply made him wrong, made him out to be the bad guy, and began to find ways to make his life miserable. Some of the ways they did this were to continually assign him the toughest hours in the local emergency room. They all began sending him every patient who came into their offices without insurance, refusing to see these people in their own offices. They also individually and together began to register complaints to the local disciplinary board. Doctors who choose to practice medicine differently than their peers will be ostracized, if not professionally destroyed. This is one more reason we cannot wait for American medicine to change itself.

Another friend of mine, Dr. Steve Johnson, called me and asked me to meet him for lunch. We had talked several times of this book, and he knew how I felt about medicine. I could tell he was upset, and in my usual style he cut to the chase. Steve was upset and in real turmoil about a doctor he had practiced with for several years. Simply put, he felt the doctor was killing people. He wanted to know what I thought about him filing a lawsuit against this doctor. He had to laugh when I burst out in a cheer. However, his agony was real. By personally taking on this doctor in a lawsuit, he had no idea what would happen to him. Another thing he had to consider is how much revenue this doctor produced for the hospital in which they both admitted patients. Steve was pretty sure the hospital would back the other doctor, not him. After much consideration and deliberation, Steve has decided to go ahead with the lawsuit. I admire Steve's courage and wonder, again, about a system that has no clear-cut, expedient ways in which to deal with doctors who are dangerous to an unsuspecting public. It is also bizarre that a good, competent doctor can do almost nothing to stop a dangerous colleague without agonizing over the consequences he may pay for blowing the whistle.

It is time to break out, to break away from the selling, brainwashing, advertising, education, and indoctrination we've all grown up with. Conventional American medicine is only one of many ways to deal with illness and disease. That they have sold us on being the main or only one simply points to the money they have spent to sell themselves.

Over time, American medicine has conditioned us to think it is normal and natural to be artificially put to sleep, cut open, have body parts cut out, and to swallow billions of pills every year. Even more damaging is that this phenomena is made to seem inevitable.

If you think you have escaped from the media blitzes and advertising done to promote American medicine, consider for a moment that Madison-Avenue advertising tells us where to live, what kind of a home to live in, where to buy our clothes, jewelry, and housecleaning supplies, what kind of a car to drive, what kind of toothpaste to buy, how our bodies and mouths are supposed to smell and what to buy to produce all those marketed results, to see your doctor for regular check-ups, just in case...blah, blah, blah.

We have come to think of medicine as an altruistic profession, yet it is full of racist and sexist practices. To even consider alternatives to our present system is antithetical to the brainwashing we have all received. The importance of seeing doctors regularly has been drummed into our heads over years. For who? For what? Simply put, to keep a high enough patient flow through doctors' offices and hospitals to keep up the doctors' incomes. The doctors and hospitals have been serving themselves, not the public.

Overkill? I don't think so. American medicine is not working. Rather than justify its continuation (even with small, incremental changes), what is needed is a complete transformation of the culture, starting with a complete restructuring of America's medical schools and the guidelines for acceptance into those schools. High scores in math and science have been the major prerequisites for admission to medical school, along with plenty of money to pay for the years of training. There is nothing inherently wrong with that if we want linear-thinkers as doctors, people who follow textbooks and mathematical equations and do as they are told, which does not require thinking. We end up with medical students and doctors who have little or no regard for the strength of the human spirit and our bodies' natural healing processes. The cost of medical training immediately eliminates a large segment of our population, hence classism in our medical system.

We need to stop supporting the medical system the way that it is now. And more importantly, everyone involved in the medical system needs to wake up to what they are doing and all that they are not providing. In order for an industry as big as American medicine is to transform itself, it has got to acknowledge how bad it really is. It has got to collectively own up to the arrogance and greed, the mistakes, the damage, and the cost in human life and suffering. It is probably not going to do that. So, it is up to us.

Finding a good, competent doctor within the existing system is a crapshoot, at best. Breaking out of this system completely is the most powerful action I could recommend. That, and beginning to trust ourselves, our innate wisdom and common sense. It could be as simple as transferring the trust we have given doctors back to ourselves. We sold out on our bodies' natural healing processes, and any possible alternatives, and caved in to the pressure of the present medical system. We gave American medicine decades of our lives without questioning them. The American medical system has made a horrifying mess, at our expense. It's time for each one of us to take our health and well-being back into our own hands—to take charge, and to stop giving any of our power away to doctors, hospitals, and drug and insurance companies. The American medical system has made victims of every one of us. An incredibly sweet ending to this mess might be to simply put American medicine, as it has been practiced for the last forty years, out of business. We could put a percentage of every facet of the medical system out of business. Or, at the very least, stop the fraud, the unnecessary tests, procedures, surgeries, prescription drugs, and grossly overpriced charges we have all been tolerating. What are we waiting for?

Because of our long years of conditioning, not running to a doctor may sound risky, but in reality it is more risky going to one. That may be very hard to hear, but your life and health are more at risk by going to most doctors. As human beings, we do what we "know" to do—it's automatic or unthinking. So, not going to a doctor may require real thinking and exploration of other alternatives.

The best analogy I can think of is this: have you ever been hungry, but nothing, in particular, sounded good? But, whatever someone else cooked and put down in front of you tasted great. You didn't have to think, you didn't have to prepare it, you probably didn't even have to move. It is in this subtle way that we have been conditioned to automatically run to the doctor. We don't have to think, we just go to them for an answer or a quick fix. We can leave it all to them. That is what we have done for decades, and they depend on us to do that. If there was a concern for wellness for us in American medicine, it would not make any kind of a difference to the doctors. Our being well provides them with no money.

There aren't enough watchdogs for the medical industry—it has become too big, and with so many different aspects, it is nearly impossible to monitor in any meaningful way. This makes it all the more important for each one of us to be accountable for our own health and well-being.

Personally, one of the irritating issues I had to deal with when I was still going to male doctors was waiting to see a doctor when I had an appointment at a specific time. After dealing with this situation several times and talking to other people about it, I came up with a solution almost accidentally. I took an afternoon off of work for a doctor's appointment. Remembering past appointments, I had the presence of mind to bring along a great book. Upon checking in with the receptionist, waiting forty minutes to be taken to an exam room, then waiting another hour and fifteen minutes, I got up, got dressed, and was about to leave the office when the doctor came in. He apologized for my wait and I let him know his apology was not enough. I told him my time was as important to me as his time was to him, that I would never be back, that I had a balance with his office of approximately seventy dollars and that he would have to deduct seventy dollars for the time I missed from work, which would zero out the balance. I told him it was more than a breakdown in communication that I was protesting, though it would have been very easy for his receptionist to let patients know he was way behind schedule and ask if anyone wanted to be rescheduled. It was more his blatant disrespect for me as a fellow human being; who the hell did he think he was that he could keep people waiting for almost two hours? This kind of treatment is inconsiderate and intolerable, yet it is a common practice. I never heard from that office again, nor did I ever get a bill. As long as we tolerate mistreatment by doctors, it will go on. As long as we think we can't make a difference, we won't.

There are simple steps you can take to get your health and well-being back under your own power. Here is a list I came up with. I am sure there are many others.

Find out if your doctor is board-certified in the field of medicine which he is practicing. Ask him, or ask to see the documentation. Some doctors have this framed on the walls in their offices. This does not guarantee anything, however. I have worked with excellent doctors who were not board-certified and with horrible, incompetent doctors that were board-certified.

Ask him if has malpractice insurance.

Ask him whether he has ever been sued, and if so, for what, and who won the suit. What happened?

Call the state licensing board to find out if your doctor has been involved in a malpractice suit.

Call your state medical disciplinary board and ask if there have been any complaints about your doctor.

How many states has he practiced in? Why did he move?

Ask him the percentage of Medicare and Medicaid patients he sees. If he doesn't see people on Medicaid or Medicare, he is in business to make a lot of money and can't be bothered with low-income people.

When you visit a doctor, does he meet with you first in his office? Or do you see him for the first time when you're undressed or on the exam table? If this is how he relates to people, don't stay for that appointment, and don't go back. Tell him why you're leaving.

How long do you have to wait in his office? If it is more

than fifteen minutes, don't wait; change to a doctor who respects your time as well as his own. Long waits in a doctor's office indicate he has a much higher regard for his time, packing his schedule to make the most amount of money, than for any interest or caring he might have for you.

Are his fees commensurate with other doctors in the area? Call around and shop prices. The doctors won't like it, but it's your money.

Never automatically pay the doctor's fees without at least attempting to negotiate the price.

If your doctor doesn't really listen to you, don't go back.

If your doctor doesn't include you in making decisions, don't go back.

Does he spend more than fifteen minutes with you? If not, don't go back.

If your doctor says you must have a particular kind of drug or treatment, find out everything you can about it before you agree to take it. Ask to look up the drug in his PDR (Physician's Desk Reference) before you leave his office. PDRs are also available in your local library. Don't take a medication until you have read about it and understand what it is and any and all side effects it may produce.

Never, never have surgery until you get at least a second opinion, if not a third and fourth opinion. Then, consider alternatives to being cut.

If you are faced with being on any kind of medication, ask your doctor for the generic prescription. Don't pay two to ten times more than necessary just to get a brand name. Part of the reason they are more expensive is because of all the advertising they do.

Find a nurse in your community or neighborhood so you have a backup to get questions answered. A nurse will be more objective, because her income is not dependent on your treatment, surgery, or drugs.

If you are seeing a doctor for pregnancy, labor, and delivery, see a woman doctor, or consider a midwife or nurse practitioner. Have your own plan for how you want your labor and delivery to go; if your doctor won't agree to it, get another doctor. It is your pregnancy and delivery, not the doctor's.

Take care of yourself through diet and exercise so you can keep your contact with the medical system to a minimum.

Ask your doctor if he is open to alternative treatments for you, such as chiropractors, diet, and exercise as a form of treatment, as well as massage therapy, herbal medicine, acupuncture, etc. If he isn't, find another doctor.

If, for any reason, you are uncomfortable with your doctor, discuss this with him, then trust yourself and your feelings, and don't go back.

If you can't understand the bills, don't pay them until you find out exactly what it is you are paying for.

Call your insurance company and find out what kinds of alternative care they provide for. If, for example you're interested in massage therapy and your insurance company doesn't cover it, request that they do and write a follow-up letter with your request.

Ask your doctor how often he has a checkup. Though they recommend regular checkups for us, many of them don't believe in them for themselves—they know they're not necessary.

Don't have any lab tests unless they are fully explained to you and you agree they need to be done. Find out the charges for these lab tests—before they are done.

Ask for the charges for any treatment, including x-rays, the doctor recommends before anything is done to you. Try negotiating a lower price. Nothing is fixed, except in the doctor's mind.

If you are diagnosed with something, go see another doctor without telling the second doctor you have already seen someone. See if their diagnoses agree. Doctors misdiagnose much more frequently than you could ever imagine.

Request that any bills you get from his or her office be in plain English so you understand them. Indecipherable bills are for the doctors or insurance companies' convenience, not yours.

Before you get sick, or need medical care, begin your own

investigation into alternatives.

Don't agree to anything—not drugs, x-rays, surgery, or treatments of any kind until you fully understand them and agree that you need them.

If you are pregnant, and for some reason you're going to a male gynecologist, find out the percentage of C-sections he performs and then call the hospital where he delivers babies and find out if the statistics he gave you were accurate.

Call your legislative representative and your congressman and request they do something about getting insurance coverage for alternative, gentler, and more natural forms of health care, including herbal medicine, chiropractic, naturopathic doctors, massage, meditation classes, and yoga.

If you are faced with surgery, have your doctor check to see which hospital has the best price. Many surgeons have privileges at multiple hospitals, but choose the hospital that ensures the surgeon more money or convenience. Paying more for a hospital, doctor, or procedure guarantees nothing.

If, for some reason, your doctor prescribes a pharmaceutical drug, ask him if he has samples he can give you. More likely than not, he will have them. You might as well have them. If they sit in the doctor's offices for too long, they will be thrown into the garbage the day after the expiration date, which is imprinted on all the labels of the boxes and bottles.

Find out your surgeon's success rate with the surgery you are facing. There is a huge disparity in percentages from doctor to doctor. General anesthetics are always life-risking. Find out about your anesthesiologist before the day of your surgery. Whether you like him or not is irrelevant when your life is in his hands. What is his success rate? How many patients have died at his hands?

Never blindly agree to anything a doctor recommends, no matter how persuasive he may be. Some of the most charming doctors are also the most lethal.

Ask for a list of five present patients of the doctor you are seeing, along with their phone numbers so you can call them to find out their relationship with, and their experience of, the doctor in question.

Start writing and calling your insurance company regularly, requesting they cover alternative forms of treatment.

If you are not interested in being kept alive on life-support machinery, make sure you have a living will made out, notarized, and an advance directive in case something happens and you cannot make any decisions. Let family members and friends know you have a living will, so they can support your decision, if the need ever arises.

Call your congressman and state representative, and let them know your views on the medical system, insurance and drug companies, etc.

Most important of all is to begin exploring alternative forms of health care so that you have something available for yourself beyond drugs and being cut.

It will take a high degree of unreasonableness on our part to stimulate any kind of change. It will be worth it. Our health and our lives are at stake.

My good friend, Janelle, went in for a routine checkup with her gynecologist. He was a well-known and respected doctor in the community. He found fibroids in her uterus and recommended she have a hysterectomy as soon as possible. She said no. She didn't have the surgery and eleven years later is in perfect health. She has not had one problem. If there was a problem it's that the doctor didn't make three thousand dollars to four thousand dollars off of my friend, and perhaps he didn't fill his quota that week with the hospital where he does surgery. Perhaps the most disturbing element of this situation is that the doctor felt he was doing his best, given his training, in recommending Janelle's uterus and ovaries be cut out. He was doing what he was trained to do, and probably, personally, he meant her no harm.

Human beings are amazing in many ways. We are adaptable and resilient. We also tolerate and put up with things. There is sometimes a fine line between the two. We have tolerated and put up with our medical system long enough. To continue to do so would be unconscionable.

American medicine is so threatened by different forms of health care, I have seen them refer to alternative forms of health care as witchcraft. American medicine doctors will ridicule and demean anything that does not fit into the old cut-and-drug paradigm—anything that takes money out of their pockets. That is how scared they are about having been found out and how committed they are to maintaining their level of income and feeling right about it.

Thirty years ago I was in a motorcycle accident, as I mentioned earlier. The left side of my hip was crushed, and I was in shock by the time I arrived at an emergency room. After the doctors were able to straighten out my legs and take x-rays (I had curled up into the fetal position), they circled around my hospital bed, with my parents in attendance, to tell me I would never walk again or be able to bear children. Or, if a miracle occurred and I did walk, it would never be without a severe limp. I remember hearing what they said, and in the next moment thinking, "Who do you guys think you are? You don't even know me. How dare you talk to me like that? I am not one of your statistics." Under doctors' orders, I stayed flat on my back for twenty-four hours a day for three months—they didn't know what else to do with me, given my injuries. Within six months, with an awesome degree of determination on my part, I was not only walking, I was on the tennis team at my high school. Imagine what might have happened if I had listened to the doctors like what they said was *the* truth. I was wiser about medicine and doctors as a kid than I was as a young adult.

We need to become active, informed, selective consumers of health care. We need to refuse to accept the doctors' words as truth. We must seek out other possibilities and begin taking care of ourselves. The American medical system is in such dire straits, they have even gotten themselves onto the nightly newscasts as special, caring consultants to our health. The first time I saw this, I laughed. Now, I don't think it is funny. Given the benefit of the doubt, they may be well meaning; however,

I find their current ploys more of the same, old, over-used tactics, new and improved, which means more of the same, old stuff. Only now they are playing on our sympathy, trying to come off as caring, concerned professionals. They must have hired great public relations firms in an attempt to clean up their public image. It is insulting to our intelligence.

I am out to break up the myths and superstitions of American medicine that surround us and blind us. I am out to create such a rift that there will be no going back to American medicine as it is dished out to the public today. I am committed to help persuade American medicine to transform itself now or disappear into antiquity to live only in museums and history books. We are worth so much more than what American medicine offers today. It is past time for a transformation of medicine and we will be the ones to make it happen. If we wait for American medicine to change itself, we will have a very long wait. If we wait for American medicine to transform itself, our children and grandchildren will be subjected to the kind of medicine that has been dished out to us—the choice of being cut or drugged, or both. If we wait for American medicine to bring integrity back into the profession, it will be a long wait and, in fact, will never happen. It is up to us.

So much of what doctors now provide is performed by nurses, nursing assistants, medical assistants, nurse anesthetists, and technicians, yet we are still billed as if the doctor himself had performed the services. Why aren't we questioning this? It may be that we have far more doctors than we need. And, it may be that the most efficient, cost-effective thing we could do is just to use doctors as the technicians they are trained to be and leave the rest to true health care providers. The medical schools and doctors won't like that, but they are a small percentage of our population.

Facing the unknown has always been a challenge for human beings. It often seems frightening. We resist change, though, in reality, everything changes. There is so much chaos and controversy surrounding the medical industry that now is the perfect time to begin exploring other possibilities. The best thing you can do is to take care of yourself and stay healthy. While you are healthy, begin exploring alternative forms of medicine—there are many available. We have been trained by the medical system, the media, and advertising to see conventional cut-and-drug treatment as our only choice; it may take a leap of faith to see alternative health care givers. Within a very short time alternative health care givers will be mainstream, accepted, and even covered by insurance companies, if insurance companies are still in the health care business. It might seem easier to leave this choice to our government, the politicians, and the medical industry itself, but that is what many of us have done for the past twenty to thirty years. That is how we got to where we are today, spending billions of dollars to be cut and drugged, with the cost of health care rapidly approaching over one *trillion* dollars a year. There is no one else who can make this choice for you—no one else can make you do anything. It is up to each one of us, and the stakes are now high enough to make the game worth playing. Each one of us needs to step up to the plate and say no. No—I will not have surgery. No—I will not take synthetic drugs. No—I will not be a patient in the assembly-line business of hospitals and doctors' clinics. My life will not be dictated by money-driven doctors and hospitals and a greed-driven medical industry.

That kind of change will take courage from each one of us. It will mean seeking something outside of tradition, outside of what is constantly advertised, outside of what is now socially and politically acceptable—and in taking action now, not someday. It will take courage, resilience, and willingness to become a student again—and to get back in touch with what works, what we can each do, personally, through diet and exercise, to be healthy and stay healthy. We must explore alternative forms of care that are available and that are gentle and noninvasive.

If you need more impetus, review the cold, hard facts of our present cut-and-drug, conventional medicine, count the number of legal drugs in your parent's home or your own home, compare the incomes of doctors to other professions, visit a nursing home, or go visit your local intensive care unit, emergency room, or any other unit in your local hospital. The next action will be easy and will seem very natural. It is time to alter our disastrous medical industry and time for a huge waking-up of the citizens of this country. We can make the difference. We do not have to tolerate the cut-and-drug approach of conventional medicine. We have tolerated it way too long.

Over the last few months I have begun my own investigation and search for alternative kinds of medicine. I am delighted with what I have found. My only regret is that I didn't begin this search twenty years ago.

From acupressurists, acupuncturists, herbalists, naturopathic physicians, massage therapists, and osteopathic physicians, to diet and nutritional therapy, exercise, yoga, counseling, therapy, hypnotherapy, the practice of martial arts, and meditation, the choices are endless, holistic, noninvasive, and healthy. I have found in alternative medicine what I expected to find in conventional medicine—a concern and caring for my whole person, not my presenting symptom.

The most basic thing to remember about alternative care is that you will not find doctors recommending them. Anything that takes money out of doctors' pockets will be discouraged by conventional practitioners. They will even say it is dangerous—like conventional medicine isn't!

There are so many alternative forms of health care available. All we have to do is give them a try. We have nothing to lose and everything to gain.

For decades now, we have been sold allopathic medicine. We have been sold that it is not only the best, but that it is the only brand of medicine that works. It is *not* the only brand of medicine, and it is *not* the best. It is only one of many forms. Conventional medicine is science based. It completely ignores the entire human side—our minds, spirits, health, healing, and prevention. It advocates popping pills and brutal, invasive surgeries. Conventional medicine has made the miracle of birth and life a medicalized, drugged event. It has made the normal end to life a prolonged, lonely agony in a cold, sterile environment. And they call this the best medicine in the world? What if it is really closer to worthless?

Allopathic medicine and the way it is practiced today has run its course. Its days are numbered. This leaves us with the possibility of true healing, health, and well-being, of honoring the wisdom of the ages and the medicines of cultures that are thousands of years old, of honoring the miracles of life and death, and of being healthy and well in between these two events.

Epilogue

Ideas are themselves substantive entities with the power to influence and even transform human life. In effect, ideas are not unlike food, vitamins, or vaccines. They invoke inherent potential for growth and development and can affect the course of evolution.

Jonas Salk

While health care reform debates continue to rage in our nation's capital and across the rest of the country, it is heartening to read of the explosion in the vast numbers of Americans seeking alternative forms of healing and health care. While lobbyists and big businesses continue to spend billions of our dollars and use the press and media for their interests, we are quietly seeking other solutions. While conventional doctors continue their cut-and-drug practice of medicine, hospital census is falling. Despite the political rhetoric, cynicism, and the resistance to universal health care with a single-payer system, our pioneering spirit is prevailing. We co-created the monster conventional medicine has become; they may not have noticed yet, but we are beginning to dismantle the monster. Sooner or later, the medical industry and our elected officials will have to wake up to the fact that it is always a mistake to underestimate American citizens. They should remember that this country was founded on a revolution.

To be treated holistically, with dignity and respect, and as partners with care givers in being well, would be revolutionary. This is what is being called for. Now.

As this book goes to press, I continue to get phone calls and letters from all over the country. Nurses are telling me over and over again that living wills are being ignored, that do-not-resuscitate (DNR) orders are being ignored, often when a patient is no longer mentally competent and can no longer fight for his or her right to die peacefully and with dignity. I have picked up my telephone to hear, "Sydne, you won't believe what we did to a patient today." A nursing supervisor in ICU told me he was completely discouraged and scared because living wills meant *nothing* to doctors. He said he would never be a patient in a hospital, ever. The nursing supervisor who trained me in ICU called yesterday to tell me it was "treacherous being a nurse." The nursing layoffs have resulted in critical care nurses being accountable for up to seven patients, not one or two. I can't even imagine. Christine went on to say that living wills are being summarily ignored, DNR orders are also being ignored, and long-term patients are common in critical care. Christine said, "Even very bright people get stupid when they have a family member or friend in ICU; they get sucked into the doctors' dramas and allow horrible medical treatments to happen even to people who are dying."

I can't help but wonder if doctors are being bought off by insurance companies. How else could they dare to ignore people's wishes? Why else would this brutality continue? Are doctors, hospitals, and insurance companies that desperate for money? Are they in a rush to make as much as possible as they see their monopoly on the medical system beginning to crumble?

Science is still somewhat revered and richly supported

with hundreds of billions of our dollars. Much of the money poured into research goes into projects like the Human Genome Project. Scientists are experimenting with gene-splicing and dicing, cloning human cells, artificial insemination, altering genes in the fetus, creating fetuses in test tubes, altering chromosomes, DNA and on and on and on. We need to choose if this is the road we want to take. In the medical system's arrogance, they haven't bothered to find out what the citizens of this country want and what we will pay for. If this kind of experimentation isn't what is being called for by us then we need to make sure our voices are heard.

To this day the reports I am getting from nurses and other health care workers express their genuine concern for patients' safety and well-being. They feel like they are caught in a time warp. The horror stories go on and on. The medical system continues to defend itself.

I don't know quite what it will take to stop the madness in our medical system, but it does have to be stopped. We are the ones to stop it.

Recommended Reading

1. *The Great White Lie*, Walt Bogdanich
2. *Confessions of a Medical Heretic*, Robert Mendolsohn, M.D.
3. *Women and Doctors*, John M. Smith, M.D.
4. *Male-Practice*, Robert Mendolsohn, M.D.
5. *Women's Health Alert*, Sidney Wolfe, M.D.
6. *Medical Nemesis*, Ivan Illich
7. *The Castrated Woman*, Naomi Miller Stokes
8. *The Great American Medical Show*, Spencer Klaw
9. *Medicine at the Crossroads*, Melvin Konner, M.D.
10. *The Doctor's Dilemma*, George Bernard Shaw
11. *The House of God*, Samuel Shem, M.D.
12. *Anatomy of an Illness*, Norman Cousins
13. *Illness as a Metaphor*, Susan Sontag

14. *Intensive Care*, Echo Heron, R.N.
15. *A Woman in Residence,* Michelle Harrison, M.D.
16. *The Beauty Myth*, Naomi Wolfe
17. *Future Shock*, Alvin Toffler
18 *Worst Pills, Best Pills*, Sidney Wolfe, M.D.
19 *Women of Power*, Laurel King
20. *The Hidden Malpractice*, Gena Correa
21. *Reforming Medicine*, Sidel and Sidel
22. *Unconditional Life*, Deepak Chopra, M.D.
23. *Quantum Healing,* Deepak Chopra, M.D.
24. *Travels*, Michael Crichton
25. *The Betrayal of Health,* Joseph Beasley, M.D.
26. *Health and Healing,* Andrew Weil, M.D.
27. *Taking Charge of Your Health,* Peter Ways, M.D.
28. *Uncommon Wisdom*, Fritjof Capra
29. *Aids: What the Government Isn't Telling You,* Lorraine Day, M.D.
30. *Savage Inequality,* Jonathon Kozol
31. *Diet for a New America*, John Robbins
32. *Eat More, Weigh Less*, Dean Ornish, M.D
34. *The Lobbyists: How the Influence Peddlers Get Their Way in Washington*, Jeffrey Birnbaum
35. *On Death and Dying*, Elisabeth Kubler-Ross, M.D.
36. *Serpents on the Staff*, Howard Wolinsky, and Tom Brune
37. *Folk Medicine*, DeForest Jarvis
38. *Your Money or Your Health,* Neil Rolde
39. *Backlash*, Susan Faludi
40. *You Can Heal Your Life*, Louise Hay
41. *You Can Heal Your Body*, Louise Hay
42. *The Fountain of Age*, Betty Friedan
43. *Ageless Body*, Timeless Mind, Deepak Chopra, M.D.
44. *Your Money or Your Life*, Donald J. Korns

Communication is welcome.

Sydne Johansen
P.O. Box 33992
Seattle, Washington 98133

About the Author

Sydne Johansen is a registered nurse and an accomplished public speaker who leads developmental and empowerment seminars across the Pacific Northwest. For six years Johansen studied both the sciences and the humanities at college; she was also a student of the martial arts. She has traveled on five continents, speaking with health-care workers and solidifying her commitment to promote effective, honest, and efficient health care. She has two children and lives in the Northwest.